TRUTH

TRUTH

Paul Horwich

Basil Blackwell

First published 1990
Reprinted 1991

Basil Blackwell Ltd
108 Cowley Road, Oxford, OX4 1JF, UK

Basil Blackwell, Inc.
3 Cambridge Center
Cambridge, Massachusetts 02142, USA

British Library Cataloguing in Publication Data

A CIP catalogue record for this book is available from the British Library.

Library of Congress Cataloging in Publication Data

Horwich, Paul.
Truth / Paul Horwich.
p. cm.
Includes bibliographical references.
ISBN 0–631–17315–3 — ISBN 0–631–17316–1 (pbk.)
1. Truth. I. Title.
BD171.H67 1990 89–29754
121—dc20 CIP

Typeset in 11 on 13 pt Plantin
by Photo·graphics, Honiton, Devon
Printed in Great Britain by Billing & Sons Ltd, Worcester

Contents

Preface

Perhaps the only points about truth on which most people could agree are, first, that each proposition specifies its own condition for being true (e.g. the proposition *that snow is white* is true if and only if *snow is white*), and, second, that the underlying nature of truth is a mystery. The general thrust of this book is to turn one of these sentiments against the other. I shall show that truth is entirely captured by the initial triviality, so that in fact nothing could be more mundane and less puzzling than the concept of truth.

This rough idea has been expressed by a fair number of eminent, twentieth-century philosophers – including Frege, Wittgenstein, Ramsey, Ayer, Strawson and Quine – and I certainly claim no originality for advocating it. But in spite of these impressive endorsements, the so-called 'redundancy theory of truth' remains unpopular; and this, I believe, is because a full case for it has never been made. The purpose of the present essay is to fill that gap. I have tried to find the best version of the idea – which I call 'minimalism' – give it a clear formulation, deal with a broad range of familiar objections, and indicate some of its philosophical consequences. I hope that this treatment will help the deflationary view of truth finally gain the acceptance that it deserves. Not only would this be good in itself, but the effect on many surrounding issues would be quite beneficial. For despite its reputation for obscurity the notion of truth is constantly employed in philosophical theory. One is tempted to rely on it in describing, for example, the aims of science, the relations of language to the world, the character of sound reasoning and the conditions for successful planning. Yet only in light of an adequate account of truth, and an appreciation of what the notion may and may not be used for, can such ideas be fully understood and evaluated.

My plan is as follows: I begin (chapter 1) by presenting the minimalist conception, and in the following chapters I refine and defend it in the course of responding to 39 alleged difficulties (which are set out in the contents). In chapter 2 I start to deal with these objections, answering questions about what is required of an adequate theory of truth and distinguishing minimalism from other deflationary accounts. In chapter 3 I argue that the role of truth in laws of cognitive science is nothing more than a display of its minimalistic function and that it should not lead us to expect there to be any theoretical analysis of truth. I then turn to the use of the concept in philosophical theory and suggest that this is often a cause of confusion: generally the issues are independent of truth, and its introduction merely muddies the waters. This is illustrated in treatments of scientific realism (chapter 4) and of problems in meta-semantics and in the philosophy of logic (chapter 5). My assumption throughout is that *propositions* are the bearers of truth and, for those readers not comfortable with this idea, chapter 6 offers some arguments in its favour. Finally, in chapter 7, I address the feeling that truths are what *correspond to reality* and I determine the extent to which this intuition may be squared with the minimalist perspective.

In order to explain this conception of *truth* I have had to say something about various other matters such as *reference*, *meaning*, *belief*, *logic*, *vagueness*, *realism* and the notion of *proposition*, and I have sometimes taken positions in these areas without providing adequate support for them. I hope that the reader will sympathize with the desire to keep this book focused and short, and will agree that the sketchiness of some of these discussions is justified by that end.

The point of view articulated here is a development of some ideas in my 'Three Forms of Realism' (published in *Synthese* in 1982), which was in turn a reaction to various writings of Michael Dummett and Hilary Putnam. Although I disagree with their conclusions about truth, I have benefited from the depth and ingenuity of their thought. It was only against this rich background that my own contrasting position could be elaborated. Another debt is to Hartry Field with whom I have had several conversations about truth in the past few years. I'm afraid I don't remember if either of us ever convinced the other of anything, but I do remember coming away from our meetings knowing that I had been helped a great deal. Anyone interested in the issues addressed here should read his essay, 'The Deflationary Conception of Truth'. In addition I would like to thank Ned Block who saw many of my drafts and, as always, supplied lots of reasonable advice; Marcus Giaquinto who never quite accepts anything I say and thereby gets me to think of better arguments; George Boolos and Dick Cartwright who helped me grapple with the foundations of logic and the early views of Moore and Russell; Jerry Katz, Tom Kuhn and Massimo Piattelli-Palmarini who pushed me to sort out my thoughts about propositions; Tyler Burge, Frank Jackson and Bob Stalnaker whose various sensible observations saved me from several wrong turns; and fellow deflationists Arthur ('The Natural Ontological Attitude') Fine and Mike ('Do We (Epistemologists) Need a Theory of Truth?') Williams who are thinking and working along similar lines and with whom I have enjoyed many fruitful and friendly discussions. I wrote the penultimate draft of this book while I was in France in the autumn of 1988, and I would like to thank the members of the *Centre de Récherche en Epistemologie Appliquée* for their hospitality, and the United States National Science Foundation for financial support during that period. The analytic philosophers in Paris with whom I discussed the project – especially Dick Carter, Pierre Jacob, François Recanati, Dan Sperber and Bill Ulrich – provided an excellent intellectual environment, and their acute and informed criticism has made this essay much less unsatisfactory than it would otherwise have been.

1

The Minimal Theory

A Sketch of the Minimalist Conception

'What is truth?' we sometimes ask – but the question tends to be rhetorical, conveying the somewhat defeatist idea that a good answer, if indeed there is such a thing, will be so subtle, so profound and so hard to find, that to look for one would surely be a waste of time. The daunting aura of depth and difficulty which surrounds this concept is perfectly understandable. For on the one hand the notion of truth pervades philosophical theorizing about the basic nature and norms of thought and action – e.g. '*truth* is the aim of science'; '*true* beliefs facilitate successful behaviour'; '*truth* is preserved in valid reasoning'; 'to understand a sentence is to know which circumstances would make it *true*'; 'evaluative assertions can be neither *true* nor false'. So insight into the underlying essence of truth promises, by helping us assess and explain such principles, to shed light on just about the whole of our conceptual scheme. But, on the other hand, this very depth can suggest that in inquiring into the nature of truth we have run up against the limits of analysis; and indeed it will be widely agreed that hardly any progress has been made towards achieving the insight we seem to need. The common-sense notion that truth is a kind of 'correspondence with the facts' has never been worked out to anyone's satisfaction. Even its advocates would concede that it remains little more than a vague, guiding intuition. But the traditional alternatives – equations of truth with 'membership in a coherent system of beliefs', or 'what would be verified in ideal conditions', or 'suitability as a basis for action' – have always looked unlikely to work, precisely because they don't accommodate the 'correspondence' intuition and this air of implausibility is substantiated in straightforward counterexamples. Hence the peculiarly enigmatic character of truth: a conception of its underlying nature appears to be at once necessary and impossible.

I believe that this impression is wholly wrong and that it grows out of two related misconceptions: first, that truth *has* some hidden structure awaiting our discovery; and, secondly, that hinging on this discovery is our ability to explain central philosophical principles such as those just mentioned, and thereby to solve a host of problems in logic, semantics and epistemology.

The main cause of these misconceptions, I suspect, is linguistic analogy. Just as the predicate, 'is magnetic', designates a feature of the world, *magnetism*, whose structure is revealed by quantum physics, and 'is diabetic' describes a group of phenomena, *diabetes*, characterizable in biology, so it seems that 'is true' attributes a complex property, *truth* – an ingredient of reality whose underlying essence will, it is hoped, one day be revealed by philosophical or scientific analysis. The trouble is that this conclusion – which we tend to presuppose in the question, 'What is truth?' – is unjustified and false. An expression might have a meaning that is somewhat disguised by its superficial form – tending, as Wittgenstein warned, to produce mistaken analogies, philosophical confusion, and insoluble pseudo-problems. The word, 'exists' provides a notorious example. And we are facing the same sort of thing here. Unlike most other predicates, 'is true' is not used to attribute to certain entities (i.e. statements, beliefs, etc.) an ordinary sort of property – a characteristic whose underlying nature will account for its relations to other ingredients of reality. Therefore, unlike most other predicates, 'is true' should not be expected to participate in some deep theory of that to which it refers – a theory that goes beyond a specification of what the word means. Thus its assimilation to superficially similar expressions is misleading. The role of truth is not what it seems.

In fact the truth predicate exists solely for the sake of a certain logical need. On occasion we wish to adopt some attitude towards a proposition – for example, believing it, assuming it for the sake of argument, or desiring that it be the case – but find ourselves thwarted by ignorance of what exactly the proposition is. We might know it only as 'what Oscar thinks' or 'Einstein's principle'; perhaps it was expressed, but not clearly or loudly enough, or in a language we don't understand; or – and this is especially common in logical and philosophical contexts – we may wish to cover infintely many propositions (in the course of generalizing) and simply can't have all of them in mind. In such situations the concept of truth is invaluable. For it enables the construction of another proposition, intimately related to the one we can't identify, which is perfectly appropriate as the alternative object of our attitude.

Consider, for example

(1) What Oscar said is true.

Here we have something of the form

(2) x is F

whose meaning is such that, given further information about the identity of x – given a further premise of the form

(3) x = the proposition that p

– we are entitled to infer

(4) p.

And it is from precisely this inferential property that propositions involving truth derive their utility. For it makes them, in certain circumstances, the only appropriate objects of our beliefs, suppositions, desires, etc. Suppose, for example, I have great confidence in Oscar's judgement about food; he has just asserted that eels are good but I didn't quite catch his remark. Which belief might I reasonably acquire? Well obviously not that eels are good. Rather what is needed is a proposition from which that one would follow, given identification of what Oscar said – a proposition equivalent to

(1*) If what Oscar said is *that eels are good* then eels are good, and if he said *that milk is white* then milk is white . . . and so on;

and the *raison d'être* of the concept of truth is that it supplies us with a proposition: namely (1).

To take another example, suppose we wish to state the logical law of excluded middle:

(5) Everything is red or not red, and happy or not happy, and cheap or not cheap . . . and so on.

Our problem is to find a single, finite proposition that has the intuitive logical power of the infinite conjunction of all these instances; and the concept of truth provides a solution.

(6) Everything is red or not red,

is known to be equivalent to

(6*) The proposition *that everything is red or not red* is true.

And similarly for the other instances. Thus the infinite series of universal disjunctions may be transformed into another infinite series of claims in which the same property, *truth*, is attributed to all the members of a class of structurally similar propositional objects. And in virtue of that form the sum of *these* claims may be captured in an ordinary universally quantified statement:

(5*) Every proposition of the form ⟨everything is F or not F⟩ is true.

It is in just this role, and not as the name of some baffling ingredient of nature, that the concept of truth figures so pervasively in philosophical reflection.[1]

What permits the notion of truth to play that role is simply that, for any declarative sentence

1 Notice that one could design an alternative way of putting the things that we actually express by means of the truth predicate. With the introduction of *sentence* variables, *predicate* variables and *substitutional* quantification our thoughts could be expressed as follows:

(4) p

our language guarantees an equivalent sentence

(4*) The proposition *that p* is true,

where the original sentence has been converted into a noun phrase, 'The proposition *that p*', occupying a position open to object variables, and where the truth predicate serves merely to restore the structure of a sentence: it acts simply as a *de-nominalizor*. In other words, in order for the truth predicate to fulfil its function we must acknowledge that

(MT) The proposition *that quarks really exist* is true if and only if quarks really exist, the proposition *that lying is bad* is true if and only if lying is bad, . . . and so on;

(1**) For any sentence such that Oscar claimed that *it*, then *it*,

or in logical notation

(1***) (p)((Oscar claimed that p) → p);

and

(5**) Given any predicate, a thing is either *it* or not *it*,

or

(5***) (F)(x)(Fx & -Fx).

However the variables '*it*', 'p', and 'F', are not the usual kind which replace *noun* phrases and refer to objects. Rather, 'F' must be construed as a 'pro-predicate', and 'p' as a 'pro-sentence'. Moreover, *generalization* with respect to these variables cannot be understood in the usual way as saying that every object has a certain property, but must be construed as asserting the truth of every legitimate substitution instance. Thus (1***) means intuitively that any result of substituting an English declarative sentence for 'p' in 'Oscar claimed *that p* → p' is true.

The advantage of the truth predicate is that it allows us to say what we want without having to employ any new linguistic apparatus of this sort. It enables us to achieve the effect of generalizing substitutionally over sentences and predicates, but by means of ordinary variables (i.e. pronouns), which range over *objects*. See chapter 2, question 6 for further discussion of this point.

but nothing more about truth need be assumed. The entire conceptual and theoretical role of truth may be explained on this basis. This confirms our suspicion that the traditional attempt to discern the *essence* of truth – to analyse that special quality which all truths supposedly have in common – is just a pseudo-problem based on syntactic overgeneralization. Unlike most other properties, *being true* is insusceptible to conceptual or scientific analysis. No wonder that its 'underlying nature' has so stubbornly resisted philosophical elaboration; for there is simply no such thing.

This sort of deflationary picture is attractively demystifying.[2] Nevertheless, it has not been widely accepted, for it faces a formidable array of theoretical and intuitive objections. My aim in this book is to work out a form of the approach that is able to deal with all the alleged difficulties. Some of them expose genuine deficiencies in certain versions of the doctrine and reveal the need for a better formulation of the deflationary position. But most of the complaints have simply been given more weight than they deserve. Indeed I tend to think that the approach has been underrated more because of the sheer number of objections to it than because of their quality. Put in more positive terms, my plan is to provide a highly deflationary account of our concept of truth – but one that can nevertheless explain the role of the notion in scientific methodology and in science itself, and enable us to find answers to such questions as: In what does our grasp of truth consist? Why is it practically useful to believe the truth? Can there be, in addition, any purely intrinsic value to such beliefs? Does science aim and progress towards the truth? How does our conception of truth bear on the nature of various types of fact and on our capacity to discover them? Is truth an explanatorily vital concept in semantics or in any of the empirical sciences?

I shall start by giving what I believe is the best statement of the deflationary point of view. Because it contains no more than

2 More or less deflationary views about truth are endorsed and defended (in various forms and to various degrees) by Frege (1891, 1918), Ramsey (1927), Ayer (1935), Wittgenstein (1922, 1953), Strawson (1950) and Quine (1970). In recent years the idea has been developed by Grover, Camp and Belnap (1975), Leeds (1978), the present author (1982b), A. Fine (1984), Soames (1984), Field (1986), M. J. Williams (1986), Loar (1987), Baldwin (1988) and Brandom (1988).

what is expressed by uncontroversial instances of the equivalence schema,

(E) It is true *that p* if and only if p,

I shall call my theory of truth, '*the minimal theory*', and I shall refer to the surrounding remarks on behalf of its adequacy as '*the minimalist conception*'. With a good formulation in hand, I want to show that the standard criticisms of deflationary approaches are either irrelevant or surmountable, to display the virtues of the theory in comparison with alternatives, and, by answering the above questions, to draw out the implications of minimalism for issues in semantics, psychology and the philosophy of science. For the sake of simplicity and conformity with natural language I begin by developing the account of truth for *propositions*. However, I shall go on to argue that the minimalist conception applies equally well to the 'truth' of utterances, mental attitudes, and other types of entity.

It might be thought that minimalism is too obvious and too weak to have any significant philosophical implications. Let me try, in at least a preliminary manner, to quell this misgiving. The real proof, of course, will be in the execution of the project. We should start by distinguishing (very roughly) two types of 'philosophical implication'. First, there are general principles involving truth: for example, that verification indicates truth, and that true beliefs are conducive to successful action. And, secondly, there are solutions to philosophical problems: for example, the paradoxes of vagueness and the issue of scientific realism. According to the minimalist conception, the equivalence schema, despite its obviousness and weakness, is *not* too weak to have significant philosophical implications – at least within the first category. On the contrary, our thesis is that it is possible to explain *all* the facts involving truth on the basis of the minimal theory. This may indeed appear to be a rather tall order. But remember that most of the interesting facts to be explained concern relations between truth and certain other matters; and in such cases it is perfectly proper to make use of theories about these other matters, and not to expect that all the explanatory work be done by the theory of truth in isolation. When this methodological point is borne in mind it becomes more plausible to suppose that the explanatory duties of a theory of truth can be carried out by the minimal theory.

As for the second class of 'philosophical implication' – namely, solutions to problems – one would expect these to flow, not from the minimal theory as such (i.e. instances of the equivalence schema), but rather from the minimalist *conception* (i.e. the thesis that our theory of truth should contain nothing more than instances of the equivalence schema). Philosophical questions are typically based on confusion rather than simple ignorance. Therefore an account that makes plain the character of truth will permit a clearer view of any problems that are thought to involve truth. The account itself may well never entail, or even suggest, any solutions. But in so far as it elucidates one of the sources of confusion it will help us to untangle the conceptual knots that are generating the problems, and thereby facilitate their solution. In the limiting case, a conception of truth can achieve this result by enabling us to see that, contrary to what has been generally presupposed, the notion of truth is not even involved in the problem. The recognition that truth plays no role can be vital to achieving the clarity needed for a solution. Thus, to put the matter somewhat paradoxically, the *relevance* of a theory of truth may lie in its import regarding the *irrelevance* of truth. We shall see, I think, that this is very often the situation. Consider, for example, the debate surrounding scientific realism. It is commonly assumed that truth is an essential constituent of the problem; one sees reference to 'realist conceptions of truth' and to 'anti-realist conceptions of truth'; and questions about the meaning of theoretical assertions, our right to believe them, and what it would be for them to be true, are all lumped together as components of a single broad problem. This intertwining of philosophically crucial notions is why the realism issue has proved so slippery and tough. What I am claiming on behalf of the minimalist conception of truth is not that it, by itself, will engender realism or anti-realism; but rather that it will make it easier for us to see that the central aspects of the realism debate have nothing to do with truth. By providing this clarification of the main problems, minimalism will take us a long way toward being able to solve them.

The Space of Alternative Theories

It will help us to focus on what is at stake in accepting the minimalist conception of truth if I contrast it with some of the well known alternatives.

Correspondence

First there is the venerable notion that truth is the property of *corresponding with reality*. In its most sophisticated formulations this has been taken to mean that the truth of a statement depends on how its constituents are arranged with respect to one another and on which entities they stand for. One strategy along these lines (Wittgenstein, 1922) is to suppose that a statement as a whole *depicts* a possible fact whose constituents are referents of the statement's constituents, and that the statement is true if and only if such a fact exists. Another strategy (Austin, 1950; Tarski, 1958; Davidson, 1969) is to define truth in terms of reference and predicate-satisfaction without importing the notions of fact and structure. Either way, these correspondence theories further divide according to what is said about reference. For example, one might suppose, with Wittgenstein (1922), that it is simply indescribable; or, with Field (1972) and Devitt (1984), that reference is a naturalistic (causal) relation; or, with Quine (1970) and Leeds (1978), that it is merely a device for semantic ascent. From our minimalist point of view, the last of these ideas is along the right lines – reference and truth being parallel notions – although, as we shall argue, it is a mistake to explain truth in terms of reference.

Coherence

The second most popular view of truth is known as the coherence theory. A system of beliefs is said to be coherent when its elements are consistent with one another and when it displays a certain overall simplicity. In that case, according to the coherence theory, the whole system and each of its elements are true. Thus truth is the property of *belonging to a harmonious system of beliefs*. This line was urged by the idealists, Bradley (1914) and Blanshard (1939), embraced by Hempel (1935), as the only alternative to what he regarded as the obnoxious metaphysics of *correspondence*, and resurrected for similar reasons by Dummett (1978) and Putnam (1981) (as the 'verificationist' or 'constructivist' theory) in their identification of truth with idealized justification. What has seemed wrong with this point of view is its refusal to endorse an apparently central feature of our conception of truth, namely the possibility of there being some discrepancy between what really *is* true and what we will (or should, given all possible evidence) *believe* to be true.

Pragmatism

In the third place we have the so-called pragmatic theory of truth, devised by James (1909) and Dewey (1938), and recently elaborated by Rorty (1982) and Papineau (1987). Here truth is *utility*; true assumptions are those that work best – those which provoke actions with desirable results. From our perspective, although there is indeed an association between the truth of a belief and its tendency to facilitate successful activity, this fact is something to be *explained*, and not stipulated by the very definition of truth.

Unanalysable Quality

Fourthly – perhaps the least attractive conclusion – there is the one-time thesis of Moore (1899, 1910/11) and Russell (1904) that truth is an indefinable, inexplicable quality that some propositions simply have and others simply lack.[3] This gives a sense of impenetrable mysteriousness to the notion of truth and can be the resort only of those who feel that the decent alternatives have been exhausted.

These traditional approaches do not typically impugn the correctness of the equivalence schema,

3 For an examination of this view as it appears in the early writings of Moore and Russell see Cartwright (1987).

(E) ⟨p⟩ is true *iff* p,[4]

but question its completeness. They deny that it tells us about the *essential nature* of truth, and so they inflate it with additional content in ways that, I shall argue, are, at best, unnecessary and, at worst, mistaken. To explain this point a little further it is useful to imagine six dimensions on which alternative accounts of truth may be characterized – each dimension varying with respect to some form of theoretical commitment.

1 An account may or may not be compositional – it may or may not define the truth of an utterance or a proposition in terms of the semantic properties of its parts. For example, a theory inflated in this way might involve the principle,

(T/R) 'a is F' is true *iff* there exists an object x such that 'a' refers to x and 'F' is satisfied by x.

The minimalist policy is not to *deny* such principles relating truth, reference, and satisfaction, but to argue that our theory of truth should not contain them as *axioms*. Instead, they should be *derived* from a conjunction of the theory of truth and quite distinct minimalist theories of reference and satisfaction.

2 An account may or may not suppose that truth is a complex property – the property, for example, of *corresponding with reality*, or *being verified in ideal conditions*, or *facilitating successful behaviour*, or *having such-and-such naturalistically specified essence*. In the context of a compositional account, the parallel issue is whether *reference* and *satisfaction* are complex relational properties – according to some philosophers, reducible to *causal* notions. The minimalist denies that truth, reference, or satisfaction are complex or naturalistic properties.

3 One may or may not insist on a conceptual analysis of truth, a specification (in philosophically unproblematic terms) of the content of every statement employing the concept. Minimalism offers no such definition, and denies the need for one.

4 One may or may not attempt to formulate a non-trivial, finite theory of truth itself – a succinct body of statements about

4 I shall write '⟨p⟩' for 'the proposition that p', and 'iff' for 'if and only if'.

truth that can be tacked on to our other theories (in physics, mathematics, etc.) to enable the deduction of everything we believe about truth. According to minimalism, there is no such thing. We can say what is in the theory of truth – an infinity of biconditionals of the form, ⟨p⟩ is true *iff* p – but we cannot formulate it explicitly because there are too many axioms.

5 One may or may not propose an account which inextricably links truth with other matters: for example, assertion, verification, reference, meaning, success, or logical entailment. Minimalism involves the contention that truth has a certain purity – that our understanding of it is independent of other ideas.

6 In particular, an account of the truth of *utterances* may or may not invoke meaning-like entities such as propositions, beliefs, truth conditions, and possible states of affairs – as, for example, in

(U) Utterance x is true *iff* x expresses the proposition *that p* and the proposition *that p* corresponds to a fact.

The minimalist view of utterances does not deny that there are such things as propositions, beliefs, truth conditions and possible states of affairs. It maintains only that our conception of truth for utterances does not presuppose them.

Thus my account will take the less theoretically loaded view with respect to each of these six dimensions of commitment. The theory of truth it proposes involves nothing more than the equivalence schema; its treatment of utterances does not invoke meaning-like entities; it is non-compositional; it denies that truth and reference are complex or naturalistic properties; and it does not insist on an eliminative account of truth attributions. In this way minimalism aims for a maximally deflationary theory of truth, which, though complete, has no extraneous content – a theory about truth, the whole of truth, and nothing but truth.

I should stress that our critique of the correspondence, coherence, constructivist, pragmatist, and primitivist accounts of truth is *not* that they are false. On the contrary, it seems quite likely that carefully qualified, true versions of each of them could be concocted. The main objection is rather that none can meet the *explanatory* demands on an adequate theory of truth. Specifically, none provides a good account of why it is that instances of the equivalence schema are true. Minimalism involves a reversal of that explanatory direction. We shall find that on the basis of the equivalence axioms it is easy to see why, and in what form, the traditional principles hold. Indeed every fact about truth can be naturally derived from those biconditionals. Therefore it is they that should constitute our basic theory of truth.

Summary of Alleged Difficulties

Objections to deflationary approaches have concerned six related topics:

The Proper Formulation: It has been no easy matter to provide even a *prima facie* plausible version of such a theory of truth – something that meets the normal methodological standards of fidelity to obvious fact, simplicity, explanatory power, etc., and that is not falsified by the 'liar' paradoxes.

The Explanatory Role of the Concept of Truth: The concept of truth is apparently employed in certain forms of scientific explanation (e.g. to help account for the contribution of language use to the achievement of practical goals), and it has been argued on this basis that deflationism must be missing something – namely, the naturalistic character that provides truth with its causal properties.

Methodology and Scientific Realism: A natural (realist) view of science is that it aims for, and gradually progresses towards, the truth – a goal that exists independently of our capacity to reach it, and that we value partly for its own sake, independently of any practical benefits that might accrue. This position would seem to require a substantial notion of truth – a conception of just the sort that the deflationary point of view eschews. In other words, any deflationary account of truth would seem to entail an anti-realist perspective on science.

Meaning and Logic: A further body of objections concerns the role of truth in semantics, and the ability of any deflationary approach to explain this role. For example, it is usual to analyse *understanding* in terms of knowledge of truth conditions, to use the concepts of truth and reference to show how the meanings of sentences depend on the meanings of their parts, to suppose that truth must be a central concept in the appraisal of alternative rules of inference, and to treat various semantic phenomena (e.g. vagueness, empty names, expressive utterances) by exploiting the idea that a proposition might be neither true nor false. It is commonly assumed that deflationary theories of truth are precluded by these demands.

Propositions and Utterances: Propositions are regarded as such obscure and bizarre entities that it may seem undesirable to base an account of truth on the schematic principle,

(E) The proposition ⟨p⟩ is true *iff* p,

which presupposes them. At the same time, the natural deflationary account of truth for *utterances*, the disquotational schema,

(D) Any utterance of the sentence 'p' is true *iff* p

has difficulty with indexical expressions (try 'I am hungry'), foreign languages ('Schnee ist weiss'), and indeed with all sentence-tokens whose truth or falsity depends on the context in which they are produced.

The 'Correspondence' Intuition: The idea that a representation is made true by its correspondence to reality has great intuitive appeal, yet there appears to be no room for any such conception within the deflationary picture.

Each of these topics receives separate treatment in the following chapters. However, they need not be taken in their order of appearance. Readers unsure about what exactly the minimal theory is should certainly not miss chapter 2. But otherwise one can proceed directly to chapter 3 where some influential arguments against minimalism are rebutted and a case in favour of it is made, or chapters 4 and 5 where its implications are examined. Anyone wary of *propositions* should not delay long before looking at chapter 6, where I am hopeful their concerns will be assuaged. And those philosophers who are fond of the correspondence theory of truth should perhaps not wait until the end before reading chapter 7 and finding that most of their intuitions may be accommodated.

I have organized the above-mentioned areas of criticism into 39 specific questions and objections. In what follows I shall articulate these problems in more detail and, in each case, sketch what I think is an adequate response. What will emerge, I hope, is a view of truth that is clear, plausible, and fairly comprehensive.

2

The Proper Formulation

The conception of truth to be defended in this essay is similar in spirit to other deflationary accounts that have appeared during the past hundred years or so, maintaining, in one way or another, that truth is not a normal property and that traditional investigations into its underlying nature have been misconceived. None of these accounts, however, has won over very many adherents, and the vast majority of philosophers either still subscribe to some form of correspondence, coherence, pragmatist or primitivist picture, or else think that no decent theory has yet been made available. One cause of dissatisfaction with deflationary proposals in the literature is that they are not described fully or precisely enough to be properly evaluated. For instance, it isn't always said whether the theory concerns the nature of *truth itself*, or merely the meaning of the word 'true'. Secondly, and exacerbating the evaluation problem, is a tendency to omit any explicit statement of what a satisfactory account is supposed to do. The adequacy conditions for a theory of truth are left unclear. A third common defect of deflationary views is their commitment to certain blatantly implausible theses: for example, that *being true* is not a property at all, or that *every* instance of ' "p" is true iff p' is correct. And, in the fourth place, objections are often left standing that could in fact be rebutted: for example, that the theory fails to say *what truth is*, and that it cannot be reconciled with the *desirability* of truth. The purpose of this chapter is to reach an exact characterization of the minimalist conception and, whilst doing so, to show how to deal with some of the problems that have notoriously afflicted previous deflationary proposals.

1 Of what kinds are the entities to which truth may be attributed?

The list of candidates includes: (a) *utterances* – individual sounds and marks located in particular regions of space and time (e.g. Oscar's saying the words 'I am hungry' at midday on 1 January 1988); (b) *sentences* – types of expression in a language; syntactic forms that are exemplified by particular utterances (e.g. the English sentence 'I am hungry'); (c) *statements*, *beliefs*, *suppositions*, etc. – individual, localized actions or states of mind (e.g. Oscar's state at midday of believing that he is hungry); (d) *propositions* – the things that are believed, stated, supposed, etc; the contents of such states (e.g. *that Oscar was hungry at midday on 1 January 1988*). I shall follow ordinary language in supposing that truth is a property of propositions.[1] Thus, if we agree with Oscar, we attribute truth to *what he said*, to the proposition he asserted. Presumably the *sentence-type of English* that he used is not true; for that very sentence-type is used on other occasions to make false statements. Nor would one normally characterize the noises he made, or his belief-state, as true. These entities are more naturally described as 'expressing a truth' and 'being *of* a true proposition'. No doubt we do attribute 'truth' to statements, beliefs, suppositions, and so on; but surely what we have in mind is that the propositional objects of these linguistic and mental acts are true, and not the acts themselves.

Most of the time I will conform to this way of speaking. To some extent this decision is non-trivial; for it involves a commitment to the existence of a breed of things called 'propositions'. However, this commitment, though controversial and in need of some defence (to be supplied in chapter 6), is much less substantial than it might seem at first. For it presupposes very little about

1 In light of the location, 'It is true that p', it might be thought that a theory of the truth *predicate* would have to be supplemented with a separate theory of the truth *operator*; but this is not so. We can construe 'It is true *that p*', on a par with 'It is true, *what Oscar said*', as an application of the truth *predicate* to the thing to which the initial 'It' refers, which is supplied by the subsequent noun phrase, '*that p*'.

the *nature* of propositions. As far as the minimal theory of truth is concerned they could be composed of abstract Fregean senses, or of concrete objects and properties; they could be identical to a certain class of sentences in some specific language, or to the meanings of sentences, or to some new and irreducible type of entity that is correlated with the meanings of certain sentences. I am not saying that there is nothing to choose amongst these answers. The point is, rather, that the minimal theory does not require any particular one of them. So that someone who wishes to avoid commitment to 'propositions' of any specific sort need not on that score object to the conception of truth that will be elaborated here.

Moreover, the view that truth is not strictly speaking attributable to utterances, or to linguistic or mental acts, is not substantial and nothing of importance in what follows will depend on it. If someone holds that an utterance may be 'true', in a certain sense, then he can simply regard my claims about the property of *expressing truth* as claims about 'truth' in his sense. Similarly for those who think that a truth predicate may be applied to acts of asserting, states of believing, etc.

2 What are the fundamental principles of the minimal theory of truth?

The axioms of the theory are propositions like

(1) ⟨⟨Snow is white⟩ is true *iff* snow is white⟩

and

(2) ⟨⟨Lying is wrong⟩ is true *iff* lying is wrong⟩;

that is to say, all the propositions whose structure is

(E*) ⟨⟨p⟩ is true *iff* p⟩.[2]

2 This claim will be modified slightly in the answer to question 10 in order to accommodate the 'liar' paradoxes.

In order to arrive at this 'propositional structure' we can begin with any one of the axioms and note that it may be divided into two complex constituents. First there is a part that is itself a proposition and which appears twice. In the case of (1), this is the constituent expressible by the English words

(3) 'Snow is white',

i.e. the proposition

(4) ⟨Snow is white⟩.

And second there is the remainder of the proposition – a constituent expressed by the schematic sentence

(E) '⟨p⟩ is true *iff* p'

i.e.

(E*) ⟨⟨p⟩ is true *iff* p⟩.[3]

This second constituent is a propositional structure. It is a function from propositions to propositions.[4] Thus if E* is applied to the proposition

3 Here I am employing the convention that surrounding any expression, e, with angled brackets, '⟨' and '⟩', produces an expression refering to *the propositional constituent corresponding to e*.

4 It is possible to do without the notion of 'propositional structure'. Instead we could characterize the axioms of the minimal theory as anything that is expressed by instances of the sentence schema,

(E) ⟨p⟩ is true *iff* p.

However, the theory cannot be restricted to instantiations of (E) by *English* sentences; for presumably there are propositions that are not expressible in current English, and the question of *their* truth must also be covered. So further 'equivalence axioms' are needed, one for each unformulatable proposition.

Although we cannot now *articulate* these extra axioms (any more than we can articulate the propositions they are about), we can nevertheless *identify* them. One way of doing this is by reference to *foreign* languages. We can suppose that the theory of truth includes whatever is expressed by instances of *translations* of the equivalence schema: e.g. instantiations of

(*continued*)

(4) ⟨Snow is white⟩

it yields the axiom

(1) ⟨⟨Snow is white⟩ is true *iff* snow is white⟩;

if it is applied to the proposition

(5) ⟨Lying is wrong⟩

it yields

(2) ⟨⟨Lying is wrong⟩ is true *iff* lying is wrong⟩.

(E-f) ⟨p⟩ est vrai *ssi* p

by French sentences, instantiations of

(E-g) ⟨p⟩ ist zwar *wnn* p

by German sentences, and so on, for all languages. If it were assumed that every proposition is expressed in some language, then this would do. But we want to allow for the existence of propositions that are not yet expressible at all. To accommodate these we might suppose that every proposition, though perhaps not expressed by any *actual* sentence, is at least expressed by a sentence in some *possible* language. And we can then regard the theory of truth as whatever would be expressed by instances of translations of the equivalence schema into possible languages.

However once the need to refer to possible languages has been acknowledged, we can see that there was no reason to have brought in *actual foreign languages*. For we can make do with our own language supplemented with possible extensions of it. In other words we can characterize the 'equivalence axioms' for unformulatable propositions by considering what would result if we *could* formulate them and *could* instantiate those formulations in *our* equivalence schema. Thus we may specify the axioms of the theory of truth as what are expressed when the schema,

(E) '⟨p⟩ is true *iff* p'

is instantiated by sentences in any possible extension of English.

Alternatively, instead of identifying the axioms indirectly in terms of how they would be *expressed* we can solve the problem by directly specifying the *propositional* structure which all and only the axioms have in common. This is the strategy adopted in the text.

Indeed when applied to any proposition, y, this function yields a corresponding axiom of the minimal theory, MT. In other words the axioms of MT are given by the principle[5]

(6) For any object x: x is an axiom of the minimal theory if and only if, for some, y, when the function E^* is applied to y, its value is x.

Or in logical notation:

(6*) $(x)\ (x \text{ is an axiom of MT} \leftrightarrow (\exists y)\ (x = E^*[y]))$.

The minimal theory has several striking features – features that might at first be regarded as grounds for dissatisfaction with it. In the first place it does not say explicitly *what truth is*; it contains no principle of the form, '(x) (x is true *iff* . . . x . . .). And so one might suspect that certain general facts about truth could not be explained by the theory. Secondly, it does not mention phenomena such as reference, meaning, logical validity, assertion, and the aim of inquiry – notions whose relation to truth one might have thought any decent theory should describe. And, thirdly, although we have been able to characterize the axioms of MT (as the propositions of a certain form) we cannot explicitly formulate the theory – for two independent reasons. In the first place the number of *formulatable* axioms is too great; there are infinitely many and though each one of them can be expressed it is not possible to write down the whole collection. In the second place there are some propositions we cannot express. And for those the

5 Patrick Grim pointed out to me that the minimal theory cannot be regarded as *the set* of propositions of the form, ⟨⟨p⟩ is true *iff* p⟩; for there is no such set. The argument for this conclusion is that if there were such a set, then there would be distinct propositions regarding *each* of its subsets, and then there would have to be distinct axioms of the theory corresponding to those propositions. Therefore there would be a 1-1 function correlating the subsets of MT with some of its members. But Cantor's diagonal argument shows that there can be no such function. Therefore, MT is not a set. In light of this result, when we say things like '⟨A⟩ follows from the minimal theory' we must take that to mean, not that the relation of *following from* holds between ⟨A⟩ and a certain entity, the minimal theory. But rather that it holds between ⟨A⟩ and *some part* of the minimal theory – i.e. between ⟨A⟩ and some set of propositions of the form, ⟨⟨p⟩ is true iff p⟩.

corresponding equivalence axioms are themselves inexpressible – although, as we have seen, it is none the less possible to say what they are.

In the following few sections we shall examine our justification for concluding that MT is nevertheless the best theory of truth, and we shall see why the peculiar features of the theory should not be held against it.

3 It seems unlikely that instances of the equivalence schema could possibly suffice to explain all of the great variety of facts about truth.

The primary test of this (and any other) theory is its capacity to accommodate the phenomena in its domain. That is to say, if our theory is a good one, it will be able to account for all the facts about truth. Let me give three examples of the sort of explanation that minimalism can provide.

I From 'What Smith said was true' and 'What Smith said was that snow is white', it follows that 'Snow is white'. Given the minimal theory (MT) this fact can be explained as follows:

	(1)	(∃!x) (Smith said x & x is true)	
	(2)	(∃!x) (Smith said x & x = ⟨snow is white⟩)	
∴	(3)	⟨snow is white⟩ is true	[from 1,2]
	(4)	⟨snow is white⟩ is true *iff* snow is white	[MT]
∴	(5)	snow is white	[from 3,4][6]

6 In order to explain why '*Possibly*, snow is white' follows from 'What Smith said is *possibly* true' and 'What Smith said is that snow is white' we must assume, not merely statement (4), but rather

Necessarily, ⟨snow is white⟩ is true *iff* snow is white.

Thus it might seem that the axioms of the theory of truth should be strengthened and taken to consist of *modal* propositions of the form

⟨*Necessarily*, ⟨p⟩ is true *iff* p⟩.

An alternative strategy, however – and one that I prefer – is to keep the theory of truth un-modal and simple, and instead *derive* the necessity of its axioms

II If one proposition (materially) implies another, and the first one is true, then so is the second. Here is a minimalist explanation:

(1) We can account for each individual proposition of the form,
⟨[p & (p→q)]→q⟩ [logic]

(2) Therefore we can explain every proposition of the form,
⟨[⟨p⟩ is true & (p→q)] → ⟨q⟩ is true⟩ [from 1 and MT]

(3) Given the meaning of 'implies', we have every proposition of the form,
⟨⟨p⟩ implies ⟨q⟩ → (p→q)⟩ [premise]

(4) Therefore we have every instance of
⟨[⟨p⟩ is true & ⟨p⟩ implies ⟨q⟩] → ⟨q⟩ is true⟩ [from 2,3]

(5) Therefore every proposition of the form,
⟨[⟨p⟩ is true & ⟨p⟩ implies ⟨q⟩] → ⟨q⟩is true⟩ [from 4 and MT]
is true

III We would be inclined to endorse the following thesis: 'If all Bill wants is to have a beer, and he thinks that merely by nodding he will get one, then, if his belief is true, he will get what he wants'. This fact would be explained as follows:

We begin with the suppositions,

---

from a separate theory of necessity. This, very roughly speaking, might go as follows:

(Nec) Sentences whose *a priori* acceptance constitutes a (meaning-giving) definition of some constituent express necessary truths.

(MT*) The disposition to assert, *a priori*, all instances of '⟨p⟩ is true iff p' constitutes an implicit (meaning-giving) definition of the truth predicate.

Consequently, all instances of '⟨p⟩ is true iff p' express necessary truths. Thus we can obtain the necessity of the axioms of truth without having to build it into the theory of truth itself.

(1) $(\exists!x)$ (Bill wants x)
(2) Bill wants ⟨Bill has a beer⟩
(3) Bill believes ⟨Bill nods → Bill has a beer⟩
(4) $(\exists!x)$ (Bill believes x & x was mentioned in premise (3) & x is true)

In addition, we can make the familiar psychological assumption

(5) [Bill wants ⟨Bill has a beer⟩ & $(\exists!x)$ (Bill wants x) & Bill believes ⟨Bill nods → Bill has a beer⟩] → Bill nods [premise]
∴ (6) Bill nods [from 1,2,3,5]

Now we can also infer,

(7) ⟨Bill nods → Bill has a beer⟩ is true [from 3,4]

And we have

(8) ⟨Bill nods → Bill has a beer⟩ is true *iff* Bill nods → Bill has a beer [MT]
∴ (9) Bill nods → Bill has a beer [from 7,8]
∴ (10) Bill has a beer [from 6,9]

But again from the theory of truth,

(11) ⟨Bill has a beer⟩ is true *iff* Bill has a beer [MT]
∴ (12) ⟨Bill has a beer⟩ is true [from 10,11]
∴ (13) $(\exists!x)$ (Bill wants x & x is true) [from 1,12]

i.e. Bill gets what he wants.

And this sort of explanation may be universalized to show in general how true beliefs engender successful action.

According to the minimalist thesis, all of the facts whose expression involves the truth predicate may be explained in such a way: namely, by assuming no more about truth than instances of the equivalence schema. Further explanations of this sort, dealing with a range of philosophically interesting facts about truth, will be given as we proceed. These explanations will confirm the view that no account of the *nature* of truth, no principle of the form '(x) (x is true *iff* . . . x . . .)', is called for.

4 The minimal theory must be incomplete, for it says nothing about the relationships between truth and evidently affiliated phenomena such as verification, practical success, reference, meaning, logical validity and assertion.

A theory of any phenomenon, X, is a collection of principles (i.e. axioms and/or rules); and the theory is *good* to the extent that it captures all the facts about that phenomenon in the simplest possible way. It won't do merely to produce some set of important facts about X and call that the theory. Nor would it suffice even if *every* fact about X were explicitly listed. Rather the understanding that we want requires some account of *explanatory relationships*. We have to locate the most basic facts regarding X, from which all the others may be explained. Of course we don't expect our theory of X to do the explanatory work all by itself. It does not follow solely from the theory of electrons that electrons are smaller than elephants; we need a theory of elephants too. Our goal, then, is to find a simple theory of X which, together with our theories of other matters, will engender all the facts.

Sometimes it will turn out, for certain phenomena, X and Y, that we cannot separate two distinct theories, one for X and one for Y: the simplest adequate body of principles we can find concerns both X and Y. Consider, for example, a geometric theory about points, lines, angles, etc. This cannot be split up into a theory of points, a theory of lines, and so on. Sometimes we are forced to acknowledge that certain theoretical phenomena are, in this way, inextricably entangled with one another. And this is a significant fact about such phenomena. But when this is *not* so, when distinct theories of X and Y *can* be given, then they *should* be given, otherwise, a misleading illusion of interdependence is conveyed and the cause of simplicity and explanatory insight is poorly served.

For this reason it seems to me not merely legitimate but important to separate, if we can, what we say about truth from our theories of reference, logic, meaning, verification, and so on. No doubt there are interesting relationships between these matters. But in so far as we want to *understand* truth and the other phenomena, then our task is to *explain* the relationships between them and not merely to recognize that they exist. We must discover the simplest principles from which they can all be deduced: and simplicity is promoted by the existence of separate theories of each phenomenon. Therefore it is quite proper to explain the properties of truth by conjoining the minimal theory with assumptions from elsewhere. (Note, for example, the use of extraneous premises in the explanations in the previous section – drawn, in those cases, from psychology and logic.) The virtue of minimalism, I claim, is that *it provides a theory of truth that is a theory of nothing else, but which is sufficient, in combination with theories of other phenomena, to explain all the facts about truth.*

5 Even if the minimal theory is, in some sense, 'adequate' and 'pure', it is nevertheless unsatisfactory, being so cumbersome that it cannot even be explicitly formulated.

Presented with the minimal theory of truth one's first instinct, no doubt, is to imagine that one can surely improve on it and capture the infinity of instances of the equivalence schema in a compact formulation. However, there does not *have* to be any succinct, non-trivial theory of truth, and I shall be arguing that in fact there isn't one. Such a theory would encapsulate the properties of truth in a *finite* body of principles which would generate everything true of truth, including, at the very least, infinitely many instances of '⟨p⟩ is true *iff* p'. Moreover if it is to be non-trivial, the theory would have to subsume all these facts without the use of notions that are themselves mysterious and unexplained. But how might this be done?

One natural suggestion is the single principle:

(7) $(x)(x \text{ is true } \textit{iff } \{\exists q\}(x = \langle q \rangle \ \& \ q))$

where the curly brackets indicate *substitional quantification* over the sentences of English. But this idea fails for a couple of reasons. In the first place, the use of substitutional quantification does not square with the *raison d'être* of our notion of truth, which is to enable us to do *without* substitutional quantification.[7] In the second place, the notion of substitutional quantification is trivially interdefinable with that of truth[8] and itself requires theoretical elucidation. But what kind of theory can be given? Presumably some specification of the rules of inference that govern it: for example, a version of 'universal instantiation', which is the schematic rule:

(8)
$$\frac{\{q\}(\ldots q \ldots)}{\therefore \ldots p \ldots}$$

However, this cannot be formulated as a generalization over sentences, namely:

(9)
$$\{p\}\ \frac{\{q\}(\ldots q \ldots)}{\therefore \ldots p \ldots}$$

For there would then be no way of getting from that principle to instances such as:

(10)
$$\frac{\{q\}(\ldots q \ldots)}{\therefore \ldots \text{snow is white} \ldots}$$

Nor, on pain of circularity, could we construe it as the claim that every instance of the schema preserves *truth*. The only alternative would be to recognize that the apparently *single* rule, (8), is in fact an infinite collection of rules; one for each 'sentence plus context' that can be put in place of 'p' and '. . . . . .'. But then we are embracing an unformulatable theory after all. Nothing has been gained; yet something (i.e. the use of truth to *dispense* with substitutional quantification) has been lost. Thus it seems that the best overall theory will not involve a definition of truth in terms of substitutional quantification.[9]

7 See chapter 1, footnote 1, and question 6 of the present chapter.

8 '$\{\exists p\}(\ldots p \ldots)$' means 'Some sentence formed by replacing the "p" in ". . . p . . ." with a sentence of (some extension of) English is true.'

9 For further discussion of the policy of explaining truth in terms of substitutional quantification see Grover, Camp and Belnap (1975) and Baldwin (1989) who appear to embrace it and Forbes (1986) who rejects it.

Another tempting approach, again designed to avoid the need for infinitely many axioms, is to formulate the theory of truth as the single proposition:

(11) Every instance of '⟨p⟩ is true *iff* p' is true.

It is clear however that this will not do. For it would enable us to deduce, for example,

(12) '⟨Snow is white⟩ is true *iff* snow is white' is true.

But we would have no license to get from there to the conclusion that

(1) ⟨Snow is white⟩ is true *iff* snow is white.

To do this we would need the schematic rule of inference:

(E#) $$\frac{\langle p \rangle \text{ is true}}{\therefore p}$$

which, as we have just seen, must be regarded as an infinite collection of separate rules.

Inspired by Tarski (1958), one might think that the solution to our difficulty is to be found by defining the truth of a whole proposition in terms of the reference of its parts and how those parts are put together. But this is a vain hope. Truth and reference are closely affiliated notions, and so a theory that characterized truth in terms of reference but gave no account of reference would be unsatisfactory. But any attempt to provide such a theory re-encounters precisely the problems with which we are now struggling. For just as the theory of truth must subsume everything like

(1) ⟨Snow is white⟩ is true iff snow is white,

so any decent theory of reference would have to subsume the fact that

(13) The propositional constituent associated with the word, 'Aristotle', refers (if at all) to Aristotle.

and so on. It might be thought that in the case of reference this problem may be solved easily – by simply listing the referents of each of the finitely many primitive terms in our language. But this is not so. Just as our understanding of truth goes beyond the list of present instances of the equivalence schema and tells us that any new sentences could also be instantiated, similarly, our conception of reference goes beyond a knowledge of the referents of our current primitive vocabulary.[10] It covers a potentially infinite number of new terms. Consequently, we are pushed into formulations such as

(14) (x) (y) (x refers to y *iff*
{∃d} (x = 'd' & y = d))

where the substitutional variable, d, ranges over singular terms in possible extensions of our language. Thus we find ourselves relying again on substitutional quantification and the need to explain it with an infinite number of rules; so the reduction of truth to reference has turned out to be futile.

Let me emphasize four points about this line of thought. In the first place, exactly the same criticism applies to the project of explaining truth in terms of *predicate satisfaction*. We would need to add a theory of satisfaction that could encompass all facts like

(15) The predicate 'blue' is satisfied by blue things;

and once again no list could suffice. An adequate theory would have to contain infinitely many propositions of the form,

(16) The propositional constituent associated with the predicate 'F' is satisfied by, and only by, things that are F.

Therefore concern about the infinite character of the minimal theory of truth cannot be assuaged by explaining truth in terms of satisfaction.

10 This point is stressed by Max Black in his (1948) critique of Tarski's theory.

Secondly, these conclusions do not tell against Tarski's *own* project, which was to explicate a notion of 'true-in-L' for certain highly artificial languages, L. Each of these languages has a fixed stock of primitives, so it is possible to explicate "refers-in-L" and "satisfies-in-L" with finite lists of principles. Our project, however, is in certain respects more ambitious than Tarski's. We are aiming for a theory of 'being true' – a property which is attributed to propositions regardless of how or whether they are expressed. Similarly we are looking for a theory of 'expressing truth' – a property we may attribute to an utterance regardless of the language in which it is couched. I have been considering the possibility that someone might hope, in defining "true", to exploit the strategy that Tarski used in his definition of "true-in-L"; but this will not work – or so I have argued.

Thirdly, it might be thought that the difficulty in obtaining at a finite, compositional theory of truth stems from the implicit assumption that propositions are constructed, as Frege said, from *the senses of words* – which are entities that require some theory of reference – and that such problems do not arise if propositions are instead constructed, as Russell proposed, from concrete objects and properties. For in that case we can say

(ET) (x) (R) (S) [x is the proposition consisting of the relation, R, and the sequence, S, of objects → (x is true ↔ S exemplifies R)].

But although this may be fine as far as it goes, it does not go far enough. For it would have to be supplemented with a theory of *exemplification*; and here is where the old troubles will emerge. We shall find that separate statements are needed to cover monadic properties, dyadic relations, triadic relations, and so on. In other words the theory would look roughly as follows:

(EX) (S) (R) [S exemplifies R ↔
$(\exists x)\ (S = \langle x \rangle\ \&\ Rx)$ v
$(\exists x)\ (\exists y)\ (S = \langle x,y \rangle\ \&\ Rxy)$ v
$(\exists x)\ (\exists y)\ (\exists z)\ (S = \langle x,y,z \rangle\ \&\ Rxyz)$ v
. . . and so on . . .].

And we are not yet dealing with logically very complex cases.

Thus it isn't any easier to give a finite theory of truth if we focus on Russellian, 'concrete' propositions.

Finally, notice that no help is to be found by looking in the direction of traditional theories of truth such as the coherence and pragmatic approaches, or by entertaining some other way of identifying truth with a naturalistic property. For whatever property, F, is associated with truth, we will be able to explain instances of the equivalence schema only to the extent that we can explain instances of the schema,

(17) ⟨p⟩ is F *iff* p.

And *this* infinite theory will be no easier to encapsulate than the minimal theory.

I conclude that we should not expect to contain all instances of the equivalence schema within a finite formulation: an infinity of axioms is needed. And since this would seem to be an unavoidable feature of any adequate theory of truth, it should not be held against MT. Therefore we must acknowledge that the theory of truth cannot be explicitly formulated. The best we can do is to give an implicit specification of its basic principles.

6 If there were really no more to a complete theory of truth than a list of biconditionals like 'The proposition *that snow is white* is true if and only if snow is white', then since one could always say 'p' rather than 'the proposition *that p* is true', it would be inexplicable that our language should contain the word 'true': there would be no point in having such a notion.

This argument has already been dealt with; but it is often raised against what are sometimes called 'redundancy' accounts of truth, so let me repeat my response. First, the fact that the only applications of truth expressly contained in the theory are within propositions of the form

(E*) ⟨⟨p⟩ is true *iff* p⟩,

does not imply that the theory covers only those cases in which truth is attributed to an articulated proposition. For suppose 'Einstein's law' refers to the proposition, $\langle E = mc^2 \rangle$. In other words,

(18) $\langle E = mc^2 \rangle$ = Einstein's law.

In that case the theory of truth, which applies in the first instance to

(19) $\langle E = mc^2 \rangle$ is true,

must apply indirectly to

(20) Einstein's law is true,

from which 'is true' cannot be removed. And it is from its role in such sentences that the truth predicate gets its value. To see this, consider how we would manage without it. We would have to put the matter roughly as follows:

(21) (x) (If Einstein's law is the proposition *that* x, then x).

But this could not be construed in the usual manner. For, given the usual conventions of quantification, that sentence is ill-formed in two distinct ways: the second occurrence of 'x' is in an opaque context, beyond the reach of normal quantification; and a variable that ranges over *objects* appears in sentential positions. In order to avoid these incoherences it would be necessary to introduce a new form of quantification – substitutional quantification – that *could* legitimately govern opaque contexts and sentence positions. That is to say, we need a quantifier,

(22) {p} (. . . p . . .),

whose meaning is not

(23) Every object, p, satisfies '. . . p . . .'

but rather

(24) Every grammatical substitution of a declarative sentence of English in place of 'p' in '. . . p . . .' yields a truth.

But such a quantifier, with its special syntactic and semantic rules, would be a cumbersome addition to our language. The point of our notion of truth is that it provides a simple alternative to this apparatus. For, as I mentioned in chapter 1, the truth predicate allows any sentence to be reformulated so that its entire content will be expressed by the new subject – a singular term open to normal objectual quantification. In other words, 'p' becomes '⟨p⟩ is true'. Therefore instead of

(25) {p} (p → p)

we can say

(26) (x) (If x is a proposition of the form ⟨p → p⟩, then x is true).

Instead of

(27) {p} (If Einstein's law is the proposition *that p*, then p)

we can say

(28) (x) (If x is a proposition of the form ⟨If Einstein's law is the proposition that p, then p⟩, then x is true),

which is logically equivalent to

(29) (x) (If x = Einstein's law, then x is true).

And, in general, instead of needing the substitutionally quantified

(22) {p} (. . . p . . .)

we can make do with the ordinary, objectually quantified

(30) (x) (If x is a proposition of the form ⟨. . . p . . .⟩, then x is true),

I am not suggesting, of course, that the truth predicate was introduced *deliberately* to perform this useful function. But I *am* supposing that its usefulness, as just described, is what explains its presence. For if it were *not* valuable at all, it would presumably fall out of use. And as for alternative functions that it might have, there simply aren't any plausible candidates.

7 The minimal theory fails to specify what are *meant* by attributions of truth. It fails to provide necessary and sufficient conditions for the applicability of the truth predicate.

The second part of this point is quite correct, but does not justify the initial complaint. For it is not the case that a satisfactory characterization of the meaning of a predicate must take the form of necessary and sufficient conditions for its correct application – i.e. an explicit, eliminative *analysis*. A definition of that sort is merely one particularly simple way of specifying the proper use of a word; but we should be open to more complex ways of doing it. So the present objection presupposes needless restrictions on what sort of definition of 'true' is needed. Once these implicit constraints are loosened, the minimalist account will no longer seem inadequate.

I can perhaps clarify this response by distinguishing some different forms that a definition of 'true' might be thought to take. In the first place one might offer an *atomic definition*: that is, a definition of the familiar form,

(31) 'true' means '. . .',

supplying a synonym that would permit us to eliminate the word 'true' in a uniform way from every context in which it appears. An example of an atomic definition is the definition of 'bachelor' as 'unmarried man'. The pragmatists' identification of truth with utility has this character.

In the second place, and a little more modestly, one might offer a *contextual definition*: that is, a set of rules that would allow the conversion of any sentence containing the word 'true' into a synonymous sentence that does not contain it. A well known example of this style of definition is Russell's (1905) theory of definite descriptions:

(32) 'The F is G' means 'Some G is the same as every F',

which reduces the definite article, 'the', to the notions of predicate logic – specifically, 'some', 'every' and 'the same as'. A partial account of truth along these lines would be contained in the schema,

(E!) 'It is true that p' means 'p'.

Thirdly, one might abandon the attempt to provide the sort of account that would enable the word 'true' to be *eliminated*, and aim instead for *implicit definition*: that is, a set of principles involving the truth predicate, our commitment to which fixes its meaning. For example, it is sometimes said that the axioms of any geometry implicitly determine the meanings of the terms 'point' and 'line', at least as they are used when proving theorems of that geometry. An account of the meaning of 'true' along these lines would be given by the substitutionally quantified principle,

(E+) $\{p\}\ (x)\ (x = \langle p \rangle \rightarrow (x \text{ is true} \leftrightarrow p))$.

Finally, one might deny that the meaning of the truth predicate can be captured in our commitment to any definite body of principles. One might hold that the proper use – hence the meaning – of 'true' is given by rules with a more complex structure than simply, *Accept 'A'*. An example of this sort of *use definition* is the idea that our conception of number is determined by the disposition to accept Peano's axioms, including infinitely many instance of the induction schema,

(33) $(F(0)\ \&\ (n)\ [F\ (n) \rightarrow F\ (n+1)]) \rightarrow (n)\ F(n)$.

Another example is provided by a certain account of the meaning of counterfactual implication, namely:

(34) 'If p were true, then q would be true' is assertible to degree x *iff* it is known that x is the empirical tendency for q to be true in circumstances in which p is true and in which all the facts causally and conceptually independent of not p still obtain.

This rule characterizes a certain sense of 'If . . . , then . . .' by specifying the appropriate level of confidence for any such conditional, and without involving any principles, in the material mode, relating counterfactual dependence to other aspects of reality.

I would suggest that the truth predicate belongs in this final category. A person's understanding of the truth predicate, 'is true' – his knowledge of its meaning – consists in his disposition to accept, without evidence, any instantiation of the schema,

(E) 'The proposition *that p* is true if and only if p',

by a declarative sentence[11] of English (including any extensions of English). Thus for a normal English speaker it consists in his disposition to accept *a priori* and by stipulation

(MT) 'The proposition *that snow is white* is true iff snow is white', 'The proposition *that I am hungry* is true iff I am hungry', 'The proposition *that Paris is beautiful* is true iff Paris is beautiful', . . .'

The minimalist account of what it is to know the meaning of the truth predicate does not provide an *analysis* and does not enable us to specify in non-circular terms the *content* of attributions of truth. This is precisely what distinguishes it from traditional approaches. But it may be none the less a perfectly acceptable account of that in which our understanding consists, just so long as it is capable of explaining all pertinent linguistic behaviour –

11 Such sentences may be identified by their *meanings*. If meaning were then defined in terms of *truth* we would have a vicious circle. However, I argue in my answers to questions 22 and 32 that meaning may be explained in terms of aspects of use (including *assertibility*) that do not presuppose the notion of truth.

all our way of deploying the term 'true'.[12] The question in other words is whether we can explain, on the hypothesis that MT governs some person's use of the truth predicate, why, for example, that person should endorse an inference from 'What Oscar said is true' and 'What Oscar said is that eels are good' to 'Eels are good'; and, in general, why he uses the truth predicate in just the way that he does. This is the adequacy condition for a theory of the meaning of the truth predicate; and judging by the examples in the answers to question 3 the minimalist account would appear to satisfy it.

8 Is the minimalist conception concerned with *truth itself* or with *the word 'true'*?

It is concerned with both – and other related entities as well. However it is important to separate the different questions it addresses. Specifically we should distinguish between:

1 a theory of the *function* of the truth predicate;
2 a theory of *truth itself*;
3 a theory of the *meaning* of the word 'true';
4 a theory of what it is for someone to *understand* the word 'true';
5 a theory of what it is to have, or grasp, the *concept* of truth.

The minimalist conception bears on all of these matters.

Our theory of the function of the truth predicate is that it exists for the indirect expression of attitudes towards unarticulated propositions and as a simple alternative to sentence variables and substitutional quantification. Our theory of truth *itself* will show

12 Notice that since minimalism does not provide an explicit definition of truth, it superficially resembles Moore's (1899) view that truth is an 'inexplicable quality'. The important difference between the two accounts, however, is that minimalism nevertheless purports to give, by means of the equivalence schema, a complete account of truth and of that in which our grasp of it consists, whereas on Moore's view it is impossible to shed any light on these matters (including why it is that the equivalence schema holds) and truth remains impenetrably mysterious.

how this function is fulfilled. It is a collection of propositions – those expressed by instances of

(E) ⟨p⟩ is true *iff* p,

– and it implies (in conjunction with theories of other things) all the facts about truth. The meaning of the word 'true' is its use in our language, which is determined by our disposition to stipulate instances of the equivalence schema, (E). Thus the meaning of the word 'true' is the linguistic practice implicit in our affirmation of the theory of truth. Understanding the word 'true' is a state of mind providing the capacity to conform with this linguistic practice and helping to explain our conformity with it. Finally, our concept of truth is the central component in the state of understanding the word – that component which is independent of language and of the particular word that is employed. Thus, the minimal theory of truth will provide the basis for accounts of the meaning and function of the truth predicate, of our understanding it, and of our grasp upon the concept of truth.

9 Even if we grant that, as predicates go, the *truth* predicate is highly unusual – even if we grant that its special function is to enable us to say certain important things while avoiding new forms of quantification – it surely does not follow that *being true* is not a genuine property.

Quite right. And it is not part of the minimalist conception to maintain that truth is not a property. On the contrary, 'is true' is a perfectly good English predicate – and (leaving aside nominalistic concerns about the very notion of 'property') one might well take this to be a conclusive criterion of standing for a property of *some* sort. What the minimalist wishes to emphasize, however, is that truth is not a *complex* or *naturalistic* property but a property of some other kind. (Hartry Field suggests the term '*logical* property'.) The point behind this jargon is that different kinds of property correspond to different roles that predicates play in our language, and that unless these differences are appreciated we will be tempted to raise questions regarding one sort that can legitimately arise only in connection with another sort. A familiar example of this phenomenon derives from the predicate 'exists'. Another, more controversial case is the conflation of normative and descriptive properties. According to minimalism, we should, for similar reasons, beware against assimilating *being true* to such properties as *being turquoise*, *being a tree*, or *being made of tin*. Otherwise we will find ourselves looking for its constitutive structure, its causal behavior, and its typical manifestations – features peculiar to what I am calling '*complex*' or '*naturalistic* properties'. We will be puzzled when these expectations are inevitably frustrated, and incline to the conclusion that the nature of truth is profoundly obscure – perhaps even incomprehensible!

As I have indicated, some philosophers hold that *no* predicate refers and that properties do not exist; and, of course, from that nominalistic point of view the particular question 'whether *truth* is a property' does not arise – at least in those words. However the underlying issue is still with us in the form of whether or not applications of the truth-predicate engender *statements* about the propositions to which it is applied. The thesis that they do distinguishes the present view from certain more radical formulations of deflationism – those according to which it is a grammatical illusion to think that

(35) X is true

makes a statement of *any* kind about the proposition X. For example, it was suggested by Frege (1891, 1918), Ramsey (1927) and Ayer (1935, 1936) that the forms

(36) p

and

(37) It is true *that p*

yield the same sense no matter what English sentence is substituted for 'p'. This is appropriately referred to as 'the redundancy theory of truth' and it evidently conflicts with the view advanced here which associates a definite propositional constituent with the truth predicate – a constituent which is part of one of these propositions but not of the other. Similarly, from the present perspective we are rejecting the idea due to Strawson (1950, 1964) and Ayer (1963) that the truth predicate is not used to give descriptions or make statements about the things to which it is applied, but that it is used instead to perform quite different speech acts: endorsing, agreeing, conceding, etc.

The trouble with the 'redundancy/performative' conception is that it cannot be squared with obvious facts about the character and function of truth. It addresses only cases like

(38) ⟨Snow is white⟩ is true,

in which the truth predicate is attached to an explicitly articulated proposition. And it maintains, with a certain *prima facie* plausibility, that the whole sentence has the same sense as the constituent

(39) Snow is white.

But notice that such uses of truth have no great value: we could easily do without them. And when we turn to genuinely useful attributions, as for example in

(40) Oscar's claim is true,

the theory has nothing to say about its sense, except that the logical form is supposedly *not* what it would seem to be; i.e. not

(41) X is F.

Consequently, the redundancy theory is quite unable to account for the inference from (40) and

(42) Oscar's claim = the proposition *that snow is white*

to

(38) The proposition *that snow is white* is true,

and hence to

(39) Snow is white,

– which is precisely the sort of reasoning on which the utility of our concept of truth depends.[13] Thus the redundancy/performative theory must be rejected. No doubt we do perform all kinds of speech act (such as *agreeing* and *conceding*) with the truth predicate. But, as Warnock (1964) observed, it is best to say that we do so *by* (not *instead of*) making a statement – that is, *by* attributing the property, truth, to the proposition in question. Just as the assertion

(43) Your article is brilliant,

may be intended to achieve an effect beyond speaking the truth; so one might well have some ulterior purpose in mind in saying,

(40) Oscar's claim is true,

yet none the less be making a statement about Oscar's claim: i.e. attributing a property to it.

10 If the equivalence schema is relied on indiscriminately – if, for example, we instantiate 'This proposition is not true' – then the notorious 'liar' paradoxes will result.

Indeed – and for that reason we must conclude that permissible instantiations of the equivalence schema are restricted in some way so as to avoid paradoxical results. We know that this restriction need not be severe. It need have no bearing on the propositions of science – the vast majority of which do not themselves involve the concept of truth. The problem of giving a *constructive* account of exactly how far one can push the equivalence principle without engendering paradox is the subject of a great deal of contemporary

13 Similar objections to the redundancy theory have been made by Tarski (1943/44), Thomson (1948), Cohen (1950), Ziff (1962) and Ezorsky (1963).

research (e.g. Tarski, 1958; Kripke, 1975; Gupta, 1982) and will not be addressed in this book. Given our purposes it suffices for us to concede that certain instances of the equivalence schema are not to be included as axioms of the minimal theory, and to note that the principles governing our selection of excluded instances are, in order of priority: (a) that the minimal theory not engender 'liar-type' contradictions; (b) that the set of excluded instances be as small as possible; and – perhaps just as important as (b) – (c) that there be a constructive specification of the excluded instances that is as simple as possible.

I should emphasize that my intention in these remarks is not to disparage constructive attempts to deal with the paradoxes, or to suggest that our knowledge about truth is not deficient in the absence of such an account. My point is merely that there are manageable and philosophically fruitful problems of truth that are independent of the search for a constructive solution to the paradoxes: first, to *outline* a theory of truth; secondly, to specify what we mean by the truth predicate; thirdly, to explain its role in our conceptual scheme; and, fourthly, to say whether there is some theory of the underlying nature of truth. There is no reason to suppose that the minimalist answers that are advanced in this essay could be undermined by any particular constructive solution to the paradoxes – so we can temporarily set those problems aside.

The object of this chapter has been to specify the adequacy conditions for a complete account of truth, to suggest that these desiderata are satisfied by a certain deflationary conception of truth, called 'minimalism', and to make sure that this proposal is not confused with various superficially similar views, such as Tarski's and the redundancy/performative account. The axioms of the minimal theory are all the propositions of the form, ⟨⟨p⟩ is true *iff* p⟩ – at least, those that don't fall foul of the 'liar' paradoxes. We found some reason to believe that such a theory – weak as it is – is nevertheless strong enough to account for the conceptual utility of truth, and explain the facts in which truth is a constituent. And we saw that the single unattractive feature of the theory – its infinite list-like character – is not mitigated by accounts of truth in terms of reference or substitutional quantification. Thus we have gone some way towards justifying the minimalist conception: the view that the minimal theory is *the* theory of truth, to which nothing more should be added.

But many problems remain. For one thing, our entire discussion has taken for granted that truth is a property of *propositions*; and those philosophers suspicious of propositions will find it hard to swallow that aspect of the view. This issue is the focus of chapter 6. I have placed it towards the end because it is something of a digression and anyone who is already comfortable with propositions can manage perfectly well without it.

Another widely felt objection to the deflationary view of truth is that it cannot be squared with the *explanatory role* of the notion of truth; and I shall attempt in the next chapter to provide further support for minimalism by showing where this argument goes wrong. The basis for the objection is the idea that any law of nature relating various properties can be explained only by reference to theories that specify the underlying character of the properties involved. For example in order to say why *all emeralds are green* we need to know what it is to be an emerald and what it is to be green. And similarly, it is argued, in so far as the notion of truth is employed in the formulation of general laws, we are going to need a substantive theory of what truth is in order to explain these laws. I want to suggest on the contrary that truth appears in explanatory generalizations in precisely the role identified by the minimalist conception, and that the equivalence axioms are quite sufficient to account for them.

3

The Explanatory Role of The Concept of Truth

11 Truth has certain characteristic effects and causes. For example, true beliefs tend to facilitate the achievement of practical goals. General laws such as this call for explanation in terms of the nature of truth. Therefore there must be some account of what truth is, going beyond the minimalist story, that provides a conceptual or naturalistic reduction of this property. (Putnam, 1978; Field, 1972, 1986; Devitt and Sterelny, 1989).

As we shall see, truth does indeed enter into explanatory principles, but their validity may be understood from within the minimal theory.

Consider in the first place those of a person's beliefs of the form,

(1) ⟨If I perform action A then state of affairs S will be realized⟩.

The psychological role of such beliefs is to motivate the performance of A when S is desired. When this process takes place, and if the belief involved is true, then the desired result will in fact obtain. In other words, if I have belief (1) and desire S, then I will do A. But if my belief is true, then, given merely the equivalence axioms, it follows that if I do A then S will be realized. Therefore, by *modus ponens*, S *will* be realized; I will get what I wanted. Thus it is easy to see how the truth of beliefs of the kind in question may contribute to the fulfilment of goals. (A formal version of this explanation was given in the answer to question 3). Moreover, such beliefs are more likely to be true if they are inferred from true premises; and very little of what we believe can be definitively excluded from the prospect of entering into such inferences as a premise. Therefore it is clear, in general, how true beliefs contribute to practical success. Nothing beyond the minimal theory is called for to explain this phenomenon.

It is worth noting three features of our argument. In the first place, it does not imply that true beliefs are *always* beneficial. That would be a mistake, since there are obviously circumstances in which a false belief happens to produce the best outcome and circumstances in which the truth would be too costly to be worth finding out. The argument purports merely to articulate a certain mechanism by which true beliefs engender beneficial results, and does not deny the existence of other mechanisms, that may operate simultaneously, by which a true belief will have bad consequences. In the second place, one might be concerned that the sort of explanation in question could not be applied to foreigners. For, it might be said, the attribution of truth to a foreigner's belief would amount to the attribution of truth to the translation into English of the foreign sentence which expresses that belief; therefore in explaining the foreigner's success in terms of the truth of his beliefs, our own linguistic habits would have to be brought into the picture. And this is very counterintuitive; for surely their success has nothing to do with us. But this concern is misguided. The minimal theory does not make any claim about the *content* of attributions of truth. It must not be supposed that when we describe a foreign utterance or a foreigner's belief as true we are basically saying that its expression in English is true. Therefore the explanation of success, when applied to foreigners, does not refer to matters that are extrinsic to their culture. In the third place, notice that the essential line of explanation here is unaffected by the recognition of more complex and realistic patterns of deliberation than those we have been assuming. For example, suppose that we really act according to the principle of utility. In other words, given the choice between actions A and B, we perform the one with the greatest expected value, calculated by means of the formula,

(2) $V(x) = [V(S1).B(S1/x)] + [V(S2).B(S2/x)] + \ldots$

(where S1, S2, . . . is an exhaustive set of mutually exclusive possible outcomes; V(S1), V(S2), . . . are the values that the agent places on them; and B(S1/x), B(S2/x), . . . are his degrees of belief that each outcome will obtain given the performance of action x). To the extent that the degrees of belief are near the truth (i.e. to the extent that B(Sj/x) is high if x would in fact bring about Sj, and low if it wouldn't) then the *expected* value of each action will be close to its *actual* value (i.e. to the value of what would in fact occur if it were performed); and therefore the decision is more likely to be objectively correct.[1] Moreover, as we saw with respect to the simpler model, these beneficial consequences of truth (in the case of beliefs of the specific kind involved in deliberation), indicate that there is value in the truth of any premises from which those beliefs might be inferred.

We may conclude that the explanatory role which the concept of truth plays in the general principle, 'True beliefs facilitate successful behaviour', may be completely understood via the minimal theory. This fact tends against various anti-minimalist positions. First, it should assuage the concerns of philosophers (such as Dummett, 1959 and Wright, 1988) who think that no deflationary conception of truth could do justice to the fact that we *aim* for the truth. Secondly, it shows that the presence of truth in such general principles gives no reason to suppose (with Putnam, 1978) that the property of truth has any sort of underlying

1 To see this, suppose that the actual consequence of act x would be S1, and consider the possibility of having had degrees of belief, B*, that were closer to the truth than B are. What this means is that B*(S1/x) is closer to 1 than B(S1/x) is; but for all n≠1, B*(Sn/x) is closer to 0 than B(Sn/x) is. Thus the expected value of x would have been

$$\begin{aligned} V^*(x) &= V(S1)(B(S1/x) + e2 + e3 + e4 + \ldots) + V(S2/x)(B(S2/x) - e2) \\ &\quad + V(S3/x)(B(S3/x) - e3) + \ldots \\ &= V(S1)B(S1/x) + (e1 + e2 + e3 + \ldots)V(S1) + \\ &\quad V(S2)B(S2/x) - e2V(S2) + \\ &\quad V(S3)B(S3/x) - e3V(S3) + \ldots \end{aligned}$$

which is *between* V(S1) (the objective value of x) and V(x) (its expected value relative to the degrees of belief, B). Therefore degrees of belief closer to the truth imply expected values closer to objective ones.

structure. And third it undermines the pragmatist's impulse to ensure *by definition* the role of truth in successful activity.

12 Another lawlike generalization is that beliefs obtained as a result of certain methods of inquiry tend to be true. Again this suggests that the minimalist conception overlooks truth's causal/explanatory nature.

We are now turning from the effects of truth to its causes. Beliefs are sometimes reached in such a way as to inspire particular confidence in their truth, and in such cases our confidence is usually vindicated. Consider, for example, observations of the colours of ordinary objects in good light. Reports of such observations are generally correct; and beliefs arrived at by deductive and inductive inference from observational premises are often correct. The question is: why is this so? Why are beliefs regarding certain domains, when resulting from certain methods of inquiry, so strikingly reliable? And won't the answer reveal something important about the nature of truth?

For any observation sentence, 'O', such as 'That's red', 'The needle coincides with the spot marked with a "3" ', etc., there are circumstances, C('O'), that we take to be particularly conducive to the accurate determination of its truth value, and there are other circumstances in which, though the sentence may nevertheless be asserted or denied, there is thought to be a much higher risk of error. One of the things we are trying to explain is why it is that every instance of

(3) 'O' would be affirmed in C('O') *iff%* O*

is true (where 'p *iff%* q' means 'The probability of q given p and of p given q are both very high', and where 'O*' is *our* way of formulating the proposition expressed by 'O'.)

At the most superficial level the explanation is quite straightforward. It is a biological fact that humans *can be* educated, and a social fact that some of them *are* educated, to say 'That's red' when and only when something red is present, providing the light is good, eyes are open, etc. That is why

(4) 'That's red' would be affirmed in C ('That's red') *iff%* something red is there.

For analogous reasons, though certainly not the *same* reasons,

(5) 'That's green' would be affirmed in C('That's green') *iff%* something green is there.

And so it will go, for each instance of

(3) 'O' would be affirmed in C('O') *iff%* O*.

Each instance has its own explanation, though some of the instances share some explanatory antecedents. Taken together, these explanations show why *every* instance of (3) is true; or, in other words, why observation reports made in good conditions tend to be true. The minimal theory of truth is perfectly adequate.

Once we have explained why, in certain circumstances, observational beliefs tend to be true, it is not difficult to see why inferred beliefs are also reliable. Truth functions of observational statements (e.g. 'That's red or green') tend to be true because they are reached by deduction from observational beliefs that tend to be true. Beliefs in generalizations of the form

(6) All As are B

(where 'A' and 'B' are observation terms) are reliable because they are reached on the basis of the observation of many diverse As that are B and of no As that are not B – and it so happens that the world is uniform in this respect. Finally, consider how we might account for the reliability of certain scientific instruments. Suppose a device, I, is designed to discover whether the state of affairs in some domain, S, is S_1, S_2, . . . , S_k, . . . , or S_n; and suppose this is done by noticing whether the observable output of the instrument is O_1, O_2, . . . , O_k, . . . , or O_n, and then inferring the presence of the corresponding state – i.e. inferring

S_k from O_k. An explanation of the reliability of I might proceed from the following premises:

(7a) The use of instrument I will give rise, for some k, to the belief that O_k obtains.
(7b) If we believe that O_k obtains then O_k probably does obtain.
(7c) There is a high nomological correlation between O_k and S_k.
(7d) If we believe that O_k obtains, then we infer that S_k obtains.

From these we can infer that instrument I will probably give rise to true beliefs concerning the domain S. Again, nothing beyond the minimal account of truth is needed here.

13 A further explanatory role for truth lies in the fact that the truth of scientific theories accounts for their empirical success. (Putnam, 1978)

No doubt we often do explain the success of a theory by reference to its truth or approximate truth. We say such things as:

(8) The Special Theory enables accurate predictions because it is true,

and

(9) The electron microscope works so well because the theories on which it is based are true.

It remains to be seen, however, whether such explanatory statements provide a reason for thinking that truth has a hidden naturalistic structure, or whether they can be perfectly well accommodated by the equivalence axioms.

Of course, I urge the latter position. Consider the situation in which we know explicitly which theory we are talking about; and suppose its formulation is not very long or complicated. Suppose, for example, that the theory is simply

(10) Nothing goes faster than light.

In that case, rather than saying

(11) The theory that nothing goes faster than light works well because it is true,

we could equally well have said

(12) The theory that nothing goes faster than light works well because nothing goes faster than light.

No further explanatory depth is achieved by putting the matter in terms of truth. None the less, use of the truth predicate in this sort of context will often have a point. What it gives us is a certain economy of expression, and the capacity to make such explanatory claims even when we don't explicitly know what the theory is, or when we wish to generalize, e.g.

(13) True theories yield accurate predictions.

But these are precisely the features of truth that are central to the minimalist conception. Clearly they can provide no reason to be dissatisfied with it.

14 Even if all our general beliefs about truth are deducible from the minimal theory (suitably augmented), this does not imply that no deeper analysis of truth is desirable; for one might well hope to find something that will show *why it is* that the equivalence schema holds. (Papineau, 1991)

We can certainly entertain the possibility that the minimal theory is susceptible of explanation via some deeper account of truth. However there is excellent reason to suppose that *in fact* there is no such deeper theory.

In the first place, a scientific analysis of the usual sort is out of the question. For the axioms of the minimal theory are *a priori*, and therefore cannot be explained by *a posteriori* facts. In other words, any naturalistic reduction of truth – like the analysis of water as H_2O, heat as molecular motion, or gravity as curvature of space–time – would make an *empirical* claim about the coextensivity of truth and some property, F. Moreover, in order to yield the equivalence axioms, this claim would have to be supplemented with further *a posteriori* claims of the form, '⟨p⟩ is F *iff* p'. And such empirical hypotheses could not be part of what explains an *a priori* theory.

Secondly, the minimal theory of truth does not cry out for explanation in the way that some theories do.[2] Consider, for example, the account of chemical valance (discussed in this connection by Hartry Field, 1972) which consists in simply listing the valances of each element:

(14) (x) (y) (x is the valence of y *iff* x = 1 and y = potassium, or x = −2 and y = sulphur, or . . .)

In this case there *is* a reason to expect further reduction. For there are laws of nature about valence – laws about the relationship between the valences of elements and the proportions in which they combine – that are not explained by the list (14). And any lawlike generalization calls for explanation on pain of looking like a sheer coincidence. However the minimal theory of truth does not itself contain such laws; and it is conceded that *every* general fact about truth may be explained by the minimal theory. Thus there is nothing that should lead us either to expect or to desire a deeper explanation.

Thirdly, it is very unlikely that any analysis of truth could be found, given the following conditions of adequacy for such an analysis:

1 There would have to be a complex property, F, made up of constituents, G, G′, G″, . . . , and coextensive with truth. In other words, it would have to be that,

2 See Leeds (1978) for discussion of this point.

x is true *iff* x is F
iff x is f(G, G′, G″, . . .)

2 It would have to be known *a priori* that

(MT*) ⟨p⟩ is f(G, G′, G″, . . .) *iff* p

(otherwise MT* could not explain the minimal theory, which is *a priori*).

3 MT* would itself have to be explained by means of simple principles about the property G, plus simple principles about the property G′, etc. Otherwise, if MT* were taken as fundamental, we would be explaining the relatively simple minimal theory, in terms of the relatively complex MT* – which violates the usual canons of explanatory priority.

But there is no reason to think that these very demanding conditions can be satisfied. And this is itself a reason for thinking that they can't be.

And, fourthly, if our thesis about the *function* of truth is correct, then the minimal theory constitutes our *definition* of 'true', and consequently is simply *not open* to explanation. I have argued that the *raison d'être* of the truth predicate is to provide a device enabling us to formulate propositions that can be the objects of belief, desire, etc., in cases where the propositions of primary concern are inaccessible – or (what comes to the same thing) to allow us to formulate 'infinite conjunctions'. I argued moreover that the simplest way of obtaining such a device is to introduce a new predicate of propositions by means of the stipulation that, for any proposition ⟨p⟩, it will apply to ⟨p⟩ just in case p. But stipulated facts are not susceptible of explanation – they are profoundly unmysterious and unsurprising. So if the minimal theory is our implicit definition of 'true' there can be no deeper theory to explain it.[3]

3 Notice that these four considerations relate not merely to *truth*, but also to *reference* and *satisfaction*. We should expect no deeper analyses of any of these semantic phenomena than are provided by their minimal theories (sketched out in the answer to question 39).

It has been shown in this chapter that the existence of various scientific, explanatory generalizations, couched in terms of truth, does not call for an *analysis* of truth – a theory of its underlying structure. This is because such laws may be wholly understood on the basis merely of the equivalence axioms; moreover any explanation of *these* propositions is at best unlikely and at worst impossible. In the next chapter I turn from the scientific to the philosophical use of the notion of truth and argue in a similar vein that its scope and value are captured by the minimalist conception.

4

Methodology and Scientific Realism

A deflationary attitude towards truth is inconsistent with the ususal view of it as a deep and vital element of philosophical theory. Consequently the many philosophers who are inclined to give the notion of truth a central role in their reflections on metaphysical, epistemological and semantic problems must reject the minimalist account of its function. Conversely those who sympathize with deflationary ideas about truth will not wish to place much theoretical weight on it. They will maintain that philosophy may employ the notion only in its minimalist capacity – that is, as something enabling the formulation of certain generalizations – and that theoretical problems must be resolved without it. The latter point of view is what I will be trying to sustain in the present chapter and in the one immediately following. Here I shall try to show that the realism/anti-realism issue (together with various related questions in the philosophy of science) have nothing at all to do with truth, and that a failure to recognize this fact has stood in the way of clear thinking about those matters. And in the next chapter I shall argue more or less the same point with respect to a range of questions in semantics and in the philosophy of logic.

15 Doesn't the deflationary perspective – the renunciation of a substantive notion of truth – lead inevitably to relativism – to the idea that there is no such thing as objective correctness?

The claim that truth is not a complex or naturalistic property – that it is 'unreal' or 'insubstantial', in the sense advocated by minimalism – must not be confused with the idea that *truths* are unreal, or, in other words, that no sentence, statement or belief is ever true. The latter view might arise from an extreme form of relativism in which it is supposed that truth is 'radically perspectival' or 'contextual' or something of the sort. But this kind of theory is not at all affiliated with the minimalist conception of truth. On the contrary, the two philosophical positions tend to be opposed to one another. For it can be precisely the association of the truth predicate with some beefed-up, highly esteemed metaphysical or epistemological property – i.e. the *substantiality* of truth – that leads to the conclusion that nothing ever quite manages to be absolutely true. And conversely, the minimalist position, in so far as it makes it easy to suppose that every proposition, or its denial, is true, implies that relativism (in at least one popular formulation) is untenable. Thus the 'insubstantiality' of truth is in no way tantamount to the non-existence of truths.[1]

16 Nevertheless, isn't the minimalist perspective in some sense anti-realist? Does it not deny that scientific theories are intended to correspond to a mind-independent world?

Debate over the question 'What is realism?', can easily take on the aspect of an empty, pointless, terminological wrangle. One philosopher will identify the position with, say, an aversion to reductionism; another will complain that certain pro-reductionist positions (e.g. that the mind is merely the brain (materialism), that mathematical facts are merely logical facts (logicism)) are not intuitively anti-realistic and that certain positions that *are* anti-realistic (e.g. that the numbers are a human invention (mathematical intuitionism)) are non-reductionist; the critic may then propose an alternative definition of 'anti-realism' – say, rejection of the principle that every proposition is either true or false; but this again will fail to satisfy everyone's intuitions about when to apply

1 An argument that the minimalist conception of truth leads to relativism has been given by Putnam (1981). However, objections that I consider to be conclusive have been leveled against it by Williams (1986).

the label. Thus the process continues interminably, so that one is left wondering – since after all the words 'realism' and 'anti-realism' are terms of art – whether there is any genuine problem here at all. Wouldn't it be best to explicitly distinguish various senses of 'realism' corresponding to each of the alternative proposals, so we can begin to focus our attention on the real questions: namely, which of these so-called 'realist' positions are correct and which are not?

I think that this tempting point of view is, in fact, mistaken. Realism and anti-realism are definite and interesting philosophical stances, and the issue of what exactly they are is a substantial one. Our impression to the contrary comes partly from the fact that the answers that are usually suggested bear such little resemblance to one another, and partly from the fact that even with respect to individual philosophical positions (for example, behaviourism and intuitionism) there is no consensus about whether they should be counted as realist or not. But the explanation of all this divergence of opinion, it seems to me, is not that there is no correct definition of realism to be found, but rather that the definitions usually proposed are of completely the wrong sort.

What I have in mind can be brought out by reviewing some well known facts about how natural kinds – for example, *diseases* – are properly defined. Notorious difficulties arise if one tries to characterize a disease in terms of observable symptoms, for there will always be some that are not manifest in a few people who nonetheless have the disease, and other characteristic conditions that sometimes occur in the absense of the disease. The familiar moral is that the right way to specify the criterion for having a disease is to identify the underlying causes of its symptoms rather than the symptoms themselves. It seems to me that this moral applies reasonably well to our questions about the nature of the realism/anti-realism issue. What accounts for the endless squabbling about it is that we have been focusing our attention on the symptoms of realism and anti-realism. Not surprisingly, no definition in those terms can work. What we must do instead is think about what it is that leads people to adopt the positions we are inclined to regard as realist or anti-realist. Thus we will see what the basic conflict between realism and anti-realism really is.

And the positions – e.g. that physical objects are constructs from experience (phenomenalism), that electrons are fictional entities (instrumentalism), etc. – that we intuitively classify as realist or anti-realist will qualify as such in virtue of being adopted as a consequence of taking one side or the other on the basic issue. Notice that this analysis of the situation will immediately account for the divergence of opinion over whether certain specific theories, such as behaviourism and intuitionism, are anti-realist or not. As in the case of a disease, where a given condition may in some cases be a symptom and in another case not, a given philosophical thesis will be an anti-realist move in the case of those philosophers who embrace it for certain reasons, but not for those whose motives are quite different. Thus we might distinguish, say, between a '*realist* behaviourist' and an '*anti-realist* behaviourist': both have exactly the same view about the reducibility of mental facts to behaviour, but they diverge in their reasons for holding it.

What then *is* the essence of realism? The answer is very simple. There is a question about how it is possible for us to know of the existence of certain facts given our ordinary conception of their nature. This is because there can seem to be a tension in ordinary thinking between the metaphysical autonomy of the world (its independence of us) and its epistemological accessibility (our capacity to find out about it). The difference between a realist and an anti-realist, in a nutshell, is that the realist decides on reflection that there is actually no difficulty here – so our ordinary ideas about what we know can stand; whereas the anti-realist decides, on the contrary, that the alleged conflict is genuine and that it has certain ramifications for what we can take ourselves to know. The alternative symptoms of anti-realism are alternative views about what these ramifications are – alternative modifications of our naive view of the world and our capacity to comprehend it. Thus it is not unusual for an anti-realist with respect to some domain to embrace one of the following strategies:

(1) Deny that there are any facts of the sort at issue (e.g. formalism, instrumentalism, emotivism, relativism).
(2) Deny that we have the capacity to know such facts (e.g. scepticism, constructive empiricism).

(3) Reduce the facts in question to other facts whose epistemological status seems unproblematic (e.g. phenomenalism, behaviourism, logicism).

The central point, once again, is that none of these doctrines, nor any collection of them, is either necessary or sufficient for anti-realism. Rather, anti-realism is the view that our common-sense conception of what we know is incoherent: the supposed character of facts of a certain type cannot be reconciled with our capacity to discover them. It is in response to this view that one or another of the above doctrines may well be espoused and in such case the adoption of the doctrine qualifies as an anti-realist move.

According to this way of thinking *any* position whatsoever might count as an anti-realist move for *some* philosopher, providing that this philosopher regards the position as the proper solution to the anti-realist dilemma. Thus the class of 'possible anti-realist positions' (like the class of 'possible symptoms of diabetes') is completely uninteresting. What is of interest, however, is something we might call the class of '*natural* anti-realist positions': that is, positions which really would remove the alleged tension in our naive worldview. In other words, it is worth distinguishing, from amongst the more or less irrelevant things an anti-realist might be inclined to say, those positions that really would, if they could be adequately sustained, address the alleged dilemma.

The three strategies mentioned above clearly have this character: they are natural anti-realist positions. However, what is glaringly absent from this group is any particular thesis about the nature of *truth*. This is not of course to deny that someone might, as a matter of biographical fact, feel forced into some account of truth by the anti-realist dilemma. My claim, rather, is that any such response would be irrational. If the dilemma is real, then no theory of truth could help to resolve it.

17 But this conclusion is extremely counter-intuitive. It seems obvious that the nature of truth bears directly on the structure of reality and the conditions for comprehending it. Surely, 'truth' and 'reality' are semantically inextricable from one another; so how could one's position in the realism debate be divorced from one's conception of truth?

The term 'realism' is an over-used, under-constrained piece of philosophical jargon, and one can no doubt invent senses of it such that the minimalist approach qualifies either as 'realist' or 'anti-realist'. However, the substantial question here, as we have just seen, concerns the relation, if any, between our conception of truth and the justifiability of believing in facts that exist independently of thought or experience. And there is no relation – or so I shall argue. On the contrary, a significant source of confusion in the debates about scientific realism is the tendency to assume that the problem of truth is fundamentally involved.[2]

Anti-realism, as we have seen, consists in a perceived tension between the realist's twin, common-sense commitments to credibility and autonomy. Some anti-realist philosophers have supposed that since the facts are independent of experience they are non-existent, or at least epistemologically inaccessible to us. Thus we arrive at the sort of instrumentalism or theoretical scepticism advocated, for example, by Duhem (1954), Popper (1962), and van Fraassen (1980). Other philosophers have supposed, conversely, that since the facts are verifiable they must reduce to observation. Thus we get the sort of reductive empiricism characteristic of phenomenalism and the Vienna Circle. But none of these natural anti-realist positions is in any way affiliated with the minimalist conception of truth. In the first place, minimalism gives no reason to think that theories are constructions out of data, and is quite at home with the holistic considerations that

2 The independence of questions about truth from the traditional issues of realism was urged by Tarski (1943/44), and has recently been emphasized by Michael Devitt (1984).

have led most philosophers to reject that aspect of logical positivism. Secondly, it is perfectly consistent with the minimal account of truth to suppose that the scientific method provides us with theories that we should believe to be *true* and not merely observationally adequate. According to the deflationary picture, believing that a theory is true is a trivial step beyond believing the theory; and the justifiability of this attitude is certainly not precluded by minimalism.[3]

Not only is the minimalist conception of truth quite neutral with respect to the two central aspects of realism (namely, the questions of justified belief and empirical reducibility), but the same can be said of alternative conceptions. As we shall now see, the *choice* of a theory of truth is orthogonal to the issues surrounding realism. The theory of truth can have no definite implications for either the epistemological or the semantic component of the problem.

Consider, for example, the constructivist account, which identifies truth with a kind of demonstrability or verifiability. There is an inclination to suppose that this conception of truth immediately entails the falsity of certain forms of scepticism, and that it thereby supports the epistemological aspect of realism. At the same time it is also thought that the meanings of sentences would be given by their 'truth conditions' (in the constructivist sense); and so it seems that the content of a claim such as

(4) There are electrons

could then be nothing more than

(5) 'There are electrons' is demonstrable.

Thus the autonomy of theoretical facts would be lost, and we would have semantic anti-realism.

But both of these arguments are fallacious. In order to combat scepticism regarding some theory, T, we must be able to argue

3 In support of the anti-sceptical component of realism I have argued elsewhere (1991) that there is really no difference between *believing* a total theory and the apparently less-commital attitude towards it of *instrumental acceptance* (i.e. relying on its observable predictions).

(in the face of the underdetermination of theory by all possible data) that we are justified in believing T. Constructivism (according to Peirce, 1932/3) tells us that we can infer

(6) T is true

from the premise

(7) T will eventually be demonstrated (i.e. verified) in the limit of scientific investigation.

In Putnam's (1981) version of the doctrine, the premise should be

(8) T would be demonstrated in the course of an ideal inquiry.

However, it is not at all obvious, from the sceptic's viewpoint, that we are entitled to believe either of these premises. Moreover, even if *that* source of scepticism were removed, it would still be unclear why a justified belief that T is true should carry with it the justification to believe T. No doubt a *minimalist* can assume that the *truth* of T implies T; for that implication is implicit in what he means by 'true'. But a constructivist, on the other hand, defines truth in terms of demonstrability. For him, the equivalence schema does not hold by definition but is a substantive claim that must be supported on the basis of his theory of truth. And the possibility of such an argument is precisely what the sceptic will deny. Thus constructivism gives no easy proof of the claims to knowledge constitutive of scientific realism.

Nor does it amount to a form of anti-realism, as many writers, following Dummett (1977), have assumed. There is a tendency to confuse the following three theses:

(9) The meaning of 'p' consists in the fact that 'p' is regarded as demonstrated in such and such circumstances;

(10) ' "p" is true' means ' "p" is demonstrable';

and

(11) 'p' means ' "p" is demonstrable'.

The final thesis evidently conflicts with realism; for it reduces facts about external reality to facts about our thought and experience. However, constructivism gives us the right to nothing more than (10), and arguably (9). And these premises provide no basis for denying that scientific theories describe a mind-independent reality.[4]

A second account of truth with merely *apparent* implications for realism is the view that truth is a primitive, non-epistemic property that is grasped independently of the equivalence schema. This view seems to wear on its face the radical autonomy of theoretical facts. And, as a consequence, scepticism can appear to be unavoidable. For if the property of truth is primitive and wholly unexplainable, then we can surely have no reason to suppose that the propositions we regard as confirmed tend to have this property. But once again, these attempts to link the theory of truth with realist and anti-realist theses are misconceived. For the meaning of the word 'true' is one thing, and the meanings of theoretical terms like 'electron' and 'super-ego' are quite separate. Whatever we say about 'true' cannot determine our view on the question of whether our theoretical terminology is reducible to observational terminology. Similarly, however mysterious and inaccessible we think the property of *truth* – however hard we suppose it is to assess 'T *is true*' – we will not necessarily be saddled with scepticism; for we need not also suppose that the property of (say) *being an electron* is mysterious and inaccessible; there need be no scepticism about T itself. As before, the essential point is that any theory that defines truth *independently* of the equivalence schema, loses the right to assume without further ado that the schema holds. Therefore, relative to the conception of truth in question, problems regarding the justification of 'T is true' are not automatically linked with problems regarding the justification of T.

4 Putnam (1983, p. 280) appears to go wrong in this way when he maintains that anyone who adopts the combination of a redundancy theory of truth and an assertibility condition conception of meaning will is 'perilously close to being a solipsist of the present instant'.

18 If, as the minimal theory implies, 'truth' is not *defined* as the product of ideal inquiry, why should we believe that an ideal inquiry would provide the truth?

To regard a certain inquiry as *ideal* is to suppose that one should not question its outcome. So if an inquiry into whether or not there is life on Mars yields the result that there isn't, and if the inquiry is taken to be ideal, then we should be absolutely confident that there is no life on Mars. Moreover, given the equivalence schema, one should also be confident in the *truth* of the proposition that there is no life on Mars. Similarly, one should believe of *any* ideal inquiry that it provides the truth.[5] This is a trivial consequence of the minimal theory and the meaning of 'ideal inquiry'. Therefore constructivism is unmotivated; for what it feels the need to guarantee by *definition* may in fact be derived from the minimal theory.

Notice that there is no presumption here that *every* hypothesis is susceptible to some idealized inquiry. Therefore, although we have grounds for the schematic thesis,

(12) If ⟨p⟩ is the product of an ideal inquiry, then ⟨p⟩ is true,

the converse claim – and, *a fortiori*, the identification of truth with idealized verification – has not been supported. Indeed this identification – the constructivist theory of truth – greatly overestimates our epistemological power. For there are truths beyond the reach of even an ideal investigation. Consider the phenomena of vagueness (e.g. 'is bald' applied to a borderline case); or underdetermination of theory by data; or sentences with assertibility conditions that don't allow for conclusive verification

5 In the terminology of Putnam (1981), we are here rebutting the 'metaphysical realist' thesis that that 'truth is radically non-epistemic'. Fine; but this does not mean that we agree to incorporate epistemic ideas into the very notion of truth. Peter van Inwagen (1988) points out in a similar vein that Putnam's argument that 'a fair amount of what we believe must be true' also does not imply that truth is an epistemic concept.

(e.g. 'The probability that drug X will cure disease Y is 0.3'). Any of these phenomena might involve a proposition which is such that no ideal investigation would engender either its assertion or its denial. In that case we have

(13) It is not the case that ⟨p⟩ is verifiable and it is not the case that ⟨−p⟩ is verifiable.

But then, according to the constructivist's definition of truth, we can infer

(14) It is not the case that ⟨p⟩ is true and it is not the case that ⟨−p⟩ is true.

And by the equivalence principle

(15) $p \leftrightarrow \langle p \rangle$ is true

we get

(16) −p and − −p,

a contradiction! Thus not only is constructivism unmotivated (i.e. not needed to account for whatever correlation exists between truth and verification), it is extensionally false since it cannot acknowledge the existence of truths that are not conclusively demonstrable. One might try to argue, in response, that given a sufficiently pumped-up construal of 'ideal inquiry', there is really no need to acknowledge unverifiable truths. For it could be supposed that for every proposition, including the problematic cases just mentioned, a *sufficiently* ideal investigation would decide its truth. But although the constructivist principle may be protected against counterexample by this manoeuvre, it will then be even less appropriate than before to regard it as our basic theory of truth. For the notion of 'sufficiently ideal inquiry' will now be one that is most naturally explicated in terms of the concept of truth. Thus the constructivist principle, once it is cast into a plausible form, clearly becomes something to be derived from the minimal theory of truth, and not to be taken as explanatorily basic.

19 How is it possible, given the minimal theory, for truth to be something of intrinsic value, desirable independently of its practical utility?

To value truth is, roughly speaking, to wish for satisfaction of the schema 'p *iff* I believe p', and therefore to be committed to the techniques of investigation that will apparently achieve this result.[6] To value truth for its own sake is to desire it to some extent regardless of its compatibility with other goals. Such a value may be ethical or aesthetic; or it may be that truth is something one simply wants. These alternative possibilities are left open by the minimal theory, as is the possibility that truth *not* be valued for its own sake. Thus what follows from minimalism on this question seems to be no more and no less than the intuitive facts of the matter: namely, the truth should be pursued for its practical benefits (see section 11) and that any further interest in it is entirely optional, neither required nor prohibited.

20 How can minimalism accommodate the idea of science progressing towards the truth?

It suffices to imagine a temporal sequence of total theories T(1), T(2), . . . , T(k), . . . , T(final), becoming gradually (but not necessarily monotonically) more similar to T(final) – where T(final) is true. T(final) is a conjunction of unknown and presently inexpressible propositions. However, as we saw in the answer to question 2, this is no obstacle to applying the truth predicate. The notion of 'theoretical similarity' remains to be explained; but there is no reason to expect that this can or should be done with a high degree of precision. We can get by with our ordinary crude

6 This is a slight oversimplification in that it does not allow for *degrees* of belief. Really, what we want is, in a certain sense, to minimize the error in our plausibility judgements. If these are represented by numbers between 0 and 1, then what we want is to minimize the square difference between the probability assigned to proposition, p, and either 1 (if p is true) or 0 (if p is false). See my (1982b) for discussion of this matter, together with an argument that these desires are accommodated by the acquisition of new data.

intuitions of the extent to which two bodies of claims are similar to one another. Of course, in order to make these comparisons it is necessary that the theory formulations be to a fair degree inter-translatable (or 'commensurable' in Kuhn's (1962) terminology). I have not tried to show that this would be so. However, I am not arguing here that there actually exists progress in science; but only that a minimalist conception of truth does not stand in the way of such a thesis.[7]

21 From the perspective of the minimalist conception of truth it is impossible to produce an adequate justification of scientific methods. (Friedman 1979)

An argument that our ways of acquiring beliefs take us in the direction of *truth* might proceed on the basis of assumptions that are themselves the results of methods we are trying to justify. That is to say, an explanation of the fact that a certain scientific method M is reliable might proceed from premises of which some are believed as a consequence of employing M itself. According to Michael Friedman this sort of derivation will sometimes constitute a *justification* of the method M. He argues that – given a sufficiently substantive conception of truth – the *circularity* that is evidently involved need not be vicious. It need not render the derivation so easy to provide that it isn't worth having. After all, he says, there can be no prior guarantee that the products of M will not suggest a theory that implies M's *un*reliability. Therefore, it can be a pleasantly surprising and epistemologically significant fact regarding M if it turns out to be demonstrably reliable – even if the demonstration employs the results of M itself.

Friedman's objection to deflationism is that, from the perspective

7 Even if we give up the idea that there exists a 'final true theory' we could still make sense of a weaker version of the view that science progresses with respect to truth. We might suppose (a) that a proposition, ⟨p⟩, is *roughly true* just in case the proposition, ⟨Roughly, p⟩ is true (for example, it is roughly true that John is six feet tall when it is true that John is roughly six feet tall); (b) that later members of the possibly endless sequence of total theories tend to contain a greater number of roughly true, basic theoretical claims than earlier members; and (c) that most members of the sequence are such that the earlier members tend to be increasingly theoretically similar to it.

of such an *in*substantive conception of truth, it would be a *trivial* matter (available regardless of what one's beliefs and methods actually are) to produce demonstrations of reliability. As a consequence, these demonstrations would be quite devoid of explanatory or epistemological importance, and we would be left with no grounds for confidence in the reliability of scientific inquiry.

He reasons as follows. Suppose

(16) Method M has engendered beliefs, p_1, p_2, . . . , and p_N.

In order to derive the reliability of M it suffices to combine premise (16) and the additional premises, p_1, p_2, . . . , and p_N, that were obtained from M. From these additional premises (and the equivalence schema) we infer that

(17) 'p_1' is true,
'p_2' is true,
. . . , and
'p_N' is true.

And then, from premise (16), we get the result that M engenders true beliefs.

This pseudo-explanation is indeed worthless and provides no support whatsoever for method M. But before casting aspersions on minimalism we should consider a series of further questions,

(18) Does minimalism play any role in the above pseudo-explanation?
(19) Could there not be – consistent with minimalism – a more substantive demonstration of M's reliability?
(20) Even from the perspective of a *non*-minimalist theory of truth, could there be a telling demonstration of M's reliability?

If the answers to these questions were, respectively, yes, no and yes, then we might indeed have to concede that minimalism has unwelcome epistemological consequences. But in fact I believe that the answer to all three questions is no. In the first place, the above pseudo-justification relies merely on the equivalences that are common to all reasonable accounts of truth. Minimalism – the thesis that such biconditionals exhaust the theory of truth – plays no role and cannot be blamed. Secondly, the reliability of certain methods may well be demonstrable on the assumption of facts discovered by other methods – but *their* reliability would then be at issue. Eventually the question would arise as to whether some method (or collection of methods) is capable of justifying itself in the manner that Friedman proposes. And it seems to me that, regardless of one's theory of truth, no such justification can be given.

Here I am questioning whether it really is possible for science to undermine itself in a thoroughgoing way. I would suggest that the circular procedure envisaged by Friedman could not go *badly* wrong; and that this has nothing to do with the account of truth that is employed. I am not denying that the theories resulting from method M might fail to provide an explanation of M's reliability. For perhaps further theories are needed; or perhaps the reliability of M is extremely hard to explain. What I question is that the theories resulting from M might imply that M is *not* reliable. Consequently, since I agree that something is supported by its successful predictions only to the extent that they *might* have been mistaken, I also question whether the success of Friedman's circular *explanatory* procedure could constitute any sort of *justification* for relying on M.[8]

In order to motivate this scepticism let me consider a couple of examples. Suppose that, on the basis of observational beliefs, 0_1, 0_2, . . . , and 0_N, we were to postulate a theory T that entails that our methods of observation were very *un*reliable. In that case we would have a theory T that, on the one hand, is confirmed by the fact that it entails 0_1, 0_2, . . . , and 0_N; yet, on the other

8 Perhaps Friedman's concern is merely with the *explanation* of M's success, and not with providing reasons for confidence in it. But this interpretation of his discussion is hard to reconcile with various facts: (a) that no reason is given for thinking that a non-trivial, minimalistically acceptable *explanation* of M's reliability cannot be found; (b) that it is thought necessary to maintain that M might undermine itself; and (c) that it is thought necessary to have a conception of truth according to which it is conceivable that most of our beliefs are false.

hand, entails that a high proportion of 0_1, 0_2, . . . , and 0_N are false. Therefore T would have to be internally inconsistent, and we shouldn't have postulated it in the first place. Similarly, suppose that our theory T*, justified by induction, entails that inductive inference is unreliable. In other words:

(20) T* → Although data have conformed to T* in the past, they will not conform to T* in the future.

Again, such a theory is internally inconsistent and should not have been taken seriously in the first place.

Thus there are limits to the extent that science, rationally pursued, can invalidate itself. But this has nothing to do with the nature of truth and, in particular, is not a consequence of minimalism. Friedman suggests, on the contrary, that a *naturalistic (causal) theory of truth* would leave more room for scientific self-criticism and self-validation, for he supposes that it would open up the possibility that most of the beliefs we regard as verified will turn out not to have the naturalistic property of truth. But this is an illusion. If there were such a property – a naturalistic reduction of truth – it could be recognized as such only by means of the assumption that it *does* tend to be present in circumstances that we regard as instances of verification. If we don't impose this constraint then we violate, not merely the *minimal* theory of truth, but, in addition, any theory that respects the equivalence of 'p' and '⟨p⟩ is true'. Thus, no remotely plausible account of truth could make it conceivable that our beliefs are predominantly false and our methods of arriving at them unreliable. The limited applicability of Friedman's epistemological strategy will not be expanded by rejecting the minimal theory.[9]

Having attempted in earlier chapters to make clear and plausible the minimalist point of view, I have here begun to explore its philosophical implications, specifically with regard to the debate over realism. Not surprisingly, what I have tried to show is that our notion of truth does not occupy the central theoretical position that philosophers often assume it must occupy. Indeed many

9 For some further criticisms of Friedman's line of thought see Williams (1986).

problems are exacerbated by the conviction that truth is essentially involved and that their solution depends on finding out more about its underlying nature. We have seen on the contrary that in so far as the notion of truth is properly employed in the philosophy of science it displays no more than its minimalistic function. And in the next chapter I argue the same point with respect to a broad range of semantic questions. I shall take up (a) the nature of understanding, (b) the basis of logic, (c) empty names, (d) vagueness, and (e) the status of ethical assertion; and I shall indicate in each case how the problems become much simpler once it is acknowledged that the concept of truth should not be relied on to solve them.

5

Meaning and Logic

> **22** As Davidson (1967) has argued, understanding a sentence, say, 'Tachyons can travel back in time', is a matter of appreciating what must be the case for the sentence to be true – knowing its <u>truth condition</u>. That is to say, one must be aware that 'Tachyons can travel back in time' is true <u>iff</u> tachyons can travel back in time. Therefore it is not possible to agree with the minimalist claim that this knowledge also helps to constitute our grasp of 'is true'. For in that case we would be faced with something like a single equation and two unknowns. Rather, if knowledge of the truth conditions of 'Tachyons can travel back in time' is to constitute our understanding of that sentence then this knowledge would presuppose some pre-existing conception of truth. (Dummett, 1959; Davidson, 1984)

What is right in this point is that knowledge of the truth condition of a sentence cannot simultaneously constitute *both* our knowledge of its meaning *and* our grasp of *truth* for the sentence. What is wrong about it is its choice of the first of these options. For, on such a view, how, to begin with, do we come to know that

(M) 'Tachyons can travel back in time' is true *iff* tachyons can travel back in time?

How could this feat be accomplished? The picture that comes to mind is that we deliberately associate the sentence 'Tachyons can travel back in time' with a possible state of affairs, where the form of association is our decision to count the sentence 'Tachyons can travel back in time' as true if and only if the state of affairs obtains. But there are considerable difficulties in this position. It is surely impossible for an individual to conceive of such an explicit association unless he employs some sort of mental event – call it 'R' – to represent the possible state of affairs. And in that case two problems emerge. In the first place, it is more straightforward to represent the association of our sentence with the possible state of affairs by means of the definition

(M*) 'Tachyons can travel back in time' is to have the same meaning as 'R',

rather than by means of (M). So the notion of truth need not be involved. And in the second place, we must raise the question of what it is to provide representation 'R' with *its* meaning. In order to avoid an infinite regress it must be conceded that certain representational entities obtain their content by means other than having been explicitly associated with possible states of affairs. Yet the truth conditional approach provides no place for such alternative means. Moreover, if some cases of meaning do not arise from explicit associations with truth conditions, then why should we assume that understanding 'Tachyons can travel back in time' must have that character?

The way to avoid this mess is to recognize that while understanding a sentence does indeed usually *coincide* with an explicit knowledge of its truth condition, understanding does not *consist* in such knowledge. It consists, rather, in understanding the sentence's constituent words and syntactic structure, which, in turn, consists in knowing their contribution to the proper use (including the assertibility conditions) of all the sentences in which these ingredients occur. Once 'Tachyons can travel back in time' is understood in this way by someone with a conception of truth, then the minimalist account entails that he knows that 'Tachyons can travel back in time' is true *iff* tachyons can travel back in time – i.e. that he knows the truth condition of 'Tachyons can travel back in time'. Moreover, such knowledge can usually be attributed only to those who understand 'Tachyons can travel back in time'.[1] Thus anyone with a conception of truth who understands 'Tachyons can travel back in time' will indeed come to know its truth condition. However, contrary to what is assumed in the objection, the understanding does not derive from this knowledge.[2]

Let me stress some aspects of this position. First, the advantage of using *assertibility conditions* (or, more generally, *proper use*) in a naturalistic characterization of understanding is that it is obvious how knowledge of the former is manifested (namely, by asserting sentences in certain conditions), whereas it is not at all clear how knowledge of truth conditions is manifested; that is, unless such knowledge is construed, in the way that I have suggested, as the *product* of a knowledge of meaning (which is in turn explained via assertibility conditions) and a grasp on the concept of truth. Secondly, it is no objection to either the coherence, or the preferability, of the notion of *the assertibility conditions of an utterance* that such conditions might sometimes *include* the utterance's truth condition. For example, it might be that one of the assertibility conditions of 'The sky is blue' is that the sky be blue. This does not alter the fact that we can see how knowledge that this *is* one of the assertibility conditions may be manifested, whereas we cannot see how knowledge of its being the truth condition may be manifested. Thirdly, an analysis of *meaning* (and *truth condition*) in terms of *assertibility condition* does not imply that a sentence cannot be true without being assertible. In the first place we are not simply identifying the meaning of a sentence with its assertibility conditions. And in the second place, even if we did, the assertibility of a sentence would not follow from its truth.[3] Finally, it is sometimes claimed to be a special advantage of the 'truth conditional' analysis of meaning that it enables us to see how the meanings of composite expressions depend on the

1 But not always. Someone who does not understand German and who is told that 'Wasser ist weiss' is true iff H_2O is white, does not understand the German sentence, even though he knows its truth condition, because he does not know whether 'Wasser' means 'water' or 'H_2O'.

2 See Harman (1974, 1982) for a statement of this position. There is more about the 'use theory of meaning' in our answer to question 32.

3 For an elaboration of this point, see the discussion of scientific realism in the answers to questions 17 and 18.

meanings of their parts, and to see, therefore, how it is possible for us, with our finite minds, to understand a potential infinity of compound expressions. It should be emphasized, however, that the compositionality of meaning can equally well be accommodated within the 'use' conception of meaning. In so far as the fact that an expression has the meaning it has consists in a certain fact about its proper use, then the meaning of a complex expression will be the fact that *its* proper use is to be worked out from the facts underlying the meanings of its constituents and structure.

23 What about falsity and negation?

The simplest deflationary strategy is to define falsity as the absence of truth, as follows:

(1) (x) (x is false *iff* x is a proposition & x is not true),

or, in other words,

(2) ⟨p⟩ is false *iff* ⟨p⟩ is not true[4]

As for the word 'not', it is traditionally supposed that the best way to define both it and the other logical constants is by means of truth tables. In the case of negation, this would be

(3)

p	not p
T	F
F	T

4 One might be inclined to specify our conception of falsity in a way that more closely parallels the minimal theory of truth: i.e. via the schema

⟨p⟩ is false *iff* not p.

However, this, as it stands is somewhat obscure; for the word 'not' does not normally function as a sentence operator.
We must read it as

⟨p⟩ is false *iff* it is not the case that p

which, given the evident synonymy of 'true' and 'the case', amounts to precisely the definition in the text.

But from the perspective of minimalism, this strategy is no good. In the first place, the symbol 'not', which is allegedly defined here, does not mean the English 'not', but rather 'It is not the case that', or in other words 'It is false that' – which isn't what we wanted to define. In the second place, when truth and falsity are explicated in accordance with the minimalist proposals, the lines of the truth table are transformed into the following theses

(N) (i) p *iff* ⟨⟨p⟩ is not true⟩ is not true,
(ii) ⟨p⟩ is not true *iff* ⟨p⟩ is not true,
(iii) ⟨p⟩ is true or ⟨p⟩ is not true.

And these theses, though to some extent constraining the meaning of 'not', are not enough to fix it completely.

A complete account of the meaning of the English word, 'not', must contain fundamental facts about its proper use that are sufficient to account for our entire employment of the term. Such basic rules of use might well include: (a) the assertibility of the theorems of deductive logic (for example, '(x) (x is F or x is not F)' and the laws implicit in (N)); (b) the principle that one never assert both 'a is F' and 'a is not F'; and (c) the rule that, in the application of an observation predicate 'O' to a perceptible object, x, if 'x is O' is *not* assertible then 'x is not O' *is* assertible. The adequacy of any such account is to be judged by whether it is capable (when conjoined with facts about the proper use of other expressions) of explaining all our ways of deploying negation.

24 As Frege (1918) said, logic is the science of truth; so surely our accounts of truth and logic should be, if not identical, at least bound up with one another. Yet the minimal theory does not even enable one to prove that the principle of non-contradiction is true.

The concept of truth is involved in stating laws of logic and metalogic; for example:

(4) Every proposition of the form, ‘p → p’, is true.
(5) If a conditional and its antecedent are true, then so is its consequent.
(6) The laws of logical inference preserve truth.

Thus one easily gains the impression that truth and logic bear a peculiarly intimate relationship to one another. Indeed Frege maintained that, just as biology is the science of living things and astronomy the science of stars, so logic is the science of truth. And it is not uncommon (e.g. Dummett, 1977; Putnam, 1978) to see the competition between alternative logics described as a choice between conceptions of truth.

From the perspective of minimalism this way of thinking is incorrect. The reason that the notion of truth is heavily involved in logic is not that logic is *about* truth but simply that logic makes precisely the sort of generalization that the truth predicate enables us to formulate.

Moreover, just as we should, if possible, pull apart from one another our theories of truth and reference, so, for the same reason, we should distinguish logic from the theory of truth. One and the same theory of truth can be combined with classical logic to demonstrate, for example, that the distributive law is true, or combined with quantum logic to show that it isn’t. And just as our belief that the Principle of Relativity is true requires for its derivation assumptions from physics as well as from the theory of truth, similarly it should be quite unsurprising that in order to prove the truth of the principle of non-contradiction we need to invoke logic, and not simply the theory of truth. This means that the issue between, for example, classical and intuitionistic logic has as little to do with truth as has the issue between Newtonian and Einsteinian physics. It would be absurd to describe the latter as a conflict between Newtonian and Einsteinian conceptions of truth; and for the same reason it is wrong to think of the logical dispute as a competition between ‘the classical conception of truth’ and ‘the intuitionistic conception of truth’.

Although I use classical logic throughout this book, none of my claims about truth presupposes it. Indeed, as I have just emphasized, a central tenet of the point of view advanced here is that the theory of truth and the theory of logic have nothing to do with one another. Thus minimalism is the proper conception of truth even in the context of deviant logics such as intuitionism or quantum logic, and would not be threatened by any arguments demonstrating the preferability of non-classical rules of inference.

25 Perhaps minimalism can be squared with alternative logics; but it cannot be squared with the role that truth must play in the *foundations* of logic – in justifying one logic over another.

But this suspicion is also mistaken; for in fact the concept of truth plays no substantial role in the justification of logic. To see this consider how a system of rules of inference, L, could conceivably be justified. One strategy, it might be thought, is to specify the meanings of the logical constants by principles in which truth is the primary semantic notion – by means of truth tables – and then to show on the basis of these principles that the rules of L preserve truth. The trouble with this strategy is that it is blatantly circular; for the principles specifying the meanings of the constants are just trivial reformulations of the very rules we want to justify. For example, the classical truth table for 'and' is

(7)

p	q	p & q
T	T	T
T	F	F
F	T	F
F	F	F

which is tantamount to the rules of inference,

(7*)
$$\frac{p, q}{p \& q} \qquad \frac{p, -q}{-(p \& q)} \qquad \frac{-p, q}{-(p \& q)} \qquad \frac{-p, -q}{-(p \& q)}$$

$$\frac{\qquad}{(p \& q) \vee (-p \& q) \vee (p \& -q) \vee (-p \& -q)},$$

for the difference between them is nothing more than the equivalence principles of truth and falsity. When these rules are supplemented with the rules underlying the other constants we obtain the classical propositional calculus. Thus the truth tables are not substantially different from the rules of inference that we are trying to support, and so do not form a suitable starting point.

A second strategy for the justification of logic L would begin with the specification of the meanings of the logical constants by means of principles whose main semantic notion is something other than truth – e.g. assertibility or proof. Consider for example the intuitionistic account of disjunction:

(8) Something is a proof of 'AvB' just in case we can see that it is (or will yield) a proof of 'A' or a proof of 'B'.

One might then hope to justify logic L by showing that only proofs in L would accord with these principles. But we should appreciate two facts about this strategy.

In the first place no account of truth is involved. So there is certainly no reason here to think that something beyond the minimal theory is required in the foundations of logic. It might be thought that assumptions about truth must play a role at some stage; for isn't the whole point to show that the rules of L preserve *truth*? But even given *that* characterization of our goal, minimalism will do. If we can show that L provides the only system of rules of inference that accord with the meanings of the logical constants then we have thereby justified the rules of L. Then, if we want, we can introduce the equivalence schema to derive the conclusion that if the premises of an argument of L are true then so is the conclusion. But this final step is not needed and does not invoke anything beyond the minimal theory.

The second point about this strategy is that it suffers from the same flaw as the first strategy, in that it does not really offer a non-circular justification of logic. The principles that, for each logical constant, constrain the assertibility conditions of sentences containing it, have no epistemological priority over the rules of inference one might derive from them. Both the assertibility conditions and the basic rules of inference each formulate instructions for the proper use of the logical constants. So, in so far as meaning is use, they could equally well be regarded as specifying the meanings of the constants. And if it is legitimate to accept the principles that specify assertibility conditions without further justification, then it should be legitimate to accept the basic rules of inference in the first place.

Thus my inclination is to suppose that the principles of deductive inference are neither susceptible, nor in need, of any sort of substantive justification. For our laws of logic implicitly constrain what we mean by 'not', 'and', 'or', and so on; so it is not possible for those laws to be irrational.[5] I have not argued for this conclusion here. All I have tried to show is that alleged justifications of logic from assumptions about the meanings of the logical constants are not substantive, and anyway do not threaten the minimalist conception of truth.

5 Dummett (1977, 1978) rejects this 'implicit definition conception of logic' (IDCL) on the grounds that it implies an implausible form of holism: namely, that no sentence of the language could be understood unless the entire language were understood. His argument, as I see it, is as follows:

1. IDCL imples that we have implicitly stipulated that the truth conditions of any sentence, 'q', are to include the existence of any argument from true premises, via our rules of inference, R, to the conclusion, 'q'.
2. In particular – given an arbitrary sentence 'p' – IDCL implies that the truth conditions of 'q' include the situation in which the truth conditions of 'p' are satisfied and in which there is an argument, via R, from 'p' to 'q'.
3. Therefore knowledge of 'q''s truth conditions requires knowledge of 'p''s truth conditions.
4. To understand a sentence is to know its truth conditions.
5. Therefore understanding 'q' requires understanding 'p'.

However, (3) does not really follow from (2). For one may know what a truth condition of 'q' is (i.e. that 'p' be true) without always being able to tell whether it is satisfied. Moreover, the thesis that IDCL implies holism was, from the outset, quite implausible. For what renders the meaning of a word relatively holistic is the degree to which its definition makes reference to other meanings. So we must admit that IDCL is not completely non-holistic; for the meanings of all the logical constants are specified simultaneously. However, there is no reference, in the definition, to the meanings of any particular non-logical words.Thus it seems clear that the degree of holism implied by IDCL is fairly limited.

26 How can truth value gaps be admitted? (Dummett, 1959)

They can't be. Given any logic that licences the principle of contraposition:

(9) (a is F → a is G) →
(a is not G → a is not F),

we can go from the minimal theory of falsity

(10) ⟨p⟩ is false ↔ ⟨p⟩ is not true

to

(11) ⟨p⟩ is not false ↔ ⟨p⟩ is not not true.

Therefore

(12) ⟨p⟩ is not true and not false
→ ⟨p⟩ is not true &
⟨p⟩ is not not true.

Thus we cannot claim of a proposition that it has no truth value, for that would imply a contradiction. Moreover, given classical logic (in particular, the law of excluded middle: '(x) (Fx v −Fx)'), we can go even further, not merely refraining from the claim that some propositions are neither true nor not true, but asserting positively that every proposition is true or not – i.e. true or false.

Admittedly these results do not derive solely from the minimal theory of truth, but depend also on our having defined falsity as the absence of truth. So one might conceivably make room for propositions that are neither true nor 'false' by constructing a narrower conception of 'falsity' than the one I have endorsed. My reasons for supposing that my characterization is the right one are: first, that it conforms to ordinary usage; and second, that given the minimalist account of the *function* of the truth-predicate, it is important to distinguish merely between those propositions that are true and those that are not. According to the minimalist conception, truth-values have no theoretical role in semantics (or elsewhere) and so there can be no theoretical reason to prefer a three-way distinction.

27 But doesn't philosophy require truth value gaps in order to accommodate such phenomena as non-referring names, vagueness, the emotivist conception of ethics, etc?

These are all cases in which the misimpression that truth is a fundamental ingredient of reality has fostered the idea that it should play a substantive role in philosophical theorizing. The minimalist position, on the other hand, is that truth can play no such role, and that whenever we are tempted to give it one, the philosophical issues will be clarified and resolved by recognizing that this is a mistake.

In the first place, as Russell (1905) argued quite convincingly against Frege (1891), an atomic proposition entails that the referents of its singular terms exist: *a is F* entails that *a exists*; and in that case, it is natural to allow that if it is false that *a exists* then it is false that *a is F*. Therefore atomic propositions containing vacuous singular terms may very plausibly be regarded as *false* and don't call for truth value gaps. One way of ensuring this result is to combine Russell's (1905) theory of definite descriptions and Quine's (1953) strategy for predicatizing names, to produce logical forms that are free of singular terms. For example,

(13) Everyone has an ancestor from Atlantis,

which contains the empty name, 'Atlantis', becomes

(13*) There is a place with the property of *being-Atlantis*, and everyone has an ancestor from there,

which is uncontroversially false.

28 It is obvious that many predicates – for example, 'blue', 'small', 'bald', 'heap' – do not have definite extensions; and when such predicates are applied to certain objects the result will surely be propositions with no truth value.

We can grant that there are indeed propositions – notably those attributing vague properties to borderline cases – which should be described as 'having no determinate truth value' or 'being objectively neither true nor false'. But we are not forced, on that account, to give up the classical law of excluded middle: (x) (Fx v −Fx). After all, *classical* logic is the logic that has been extracted from ordinary linguistic practice, and ordinary language is predominantly vague; so it would be remarkable if the phenomenon of vagueness were to dictate any departure from classical logic. Nor would it be appropriate to restrict the application of classical logic to propositions with a determinate truth value. In the first place, such a strategy would not generally be workable. For sometimes the use of logic is required to see what entails a given proposition and thereby to discover whether or not it has a determinate truth value. And in that case, the proposition could be tested for its subjectability to logic only by already presupposing that it will pass the test. And, secondly, any restriction of logic to propositions that are definitely true or definitely false would conflict with the *a priori* character of logical laws, since their applicability would become contingent on the favourable outcome of empirical investigation – the determination of whether we are, or are not, dealing with a borderline case.

It seems, therefore, that the classical law of excluded middle should be retained. Moreover once we have steeled ourselves to apply this law come what may, it is not *additionally* counter-intuitive to retain also the principle of bivalence: that every proposition is true or false. On the contrary, its rejection leads quickly to contradiction, as we saw in the answer to question 26.

These considerations should dampen the urge to back away from bivalence and/or the law of excluded middle. But that urge will not be completely relieved until we have a satisfactory treatment of vagueness – one that will plainly allow those principles to be preserved. And in order to obtain such an account the crucial thing, it seems to me, is to recognize a distinction between ordinary *truth* and *determinate truth* (Field, 1986; Wright, 1987), enabling us to say that a proposition in which a vague predicate is applied to a borderline case is *not determinately true* but might none the less be *true*. A natural explication of the needed notion of determinacy may be given in terms of whether the underlying information relevant to the assessment of a proposition will actually suffice to verify or falsify it. More specifically, each proposition determines a set of observations, experiments, calculations, etc. that must be carried out to discover whether or not the proposition is true. In addition it determines how all this information must be processed in order to reach an answer. Now it sometimes happens that the underlying information is insufficient: although we do have all the facts designated as relevant by the nature of the proposition in question, those facts aren't enough; for the prescribed evaluation procedure yields no answer. In that case the proposition's truth value is indeterminate; otherwise it is determinate. Thus

(14) ⟨p⟩ is determinate,

will mean

(14*) It may be established (given knowledge of underlying conditions) whether or not p.

Therefore we have,

(15) ⟨p⟩ is determinate *iff* ⟨⟨p⟩ is true⟩ is determinate.

Consider, for example, the ascription of 'heap' to an unclear case – a little pile of sand. In accordance with classical logic

(16) It is, or is not, a heap.

However the underlying conditions – the number, size and arrangement of the grains, etc. – do not entail that it is a heap and do not entail that it isn't one. Therefore we must also say

(17) It's neither determinately a heap nor determinately not a heap.

Now we can apply the equivalence schema to (16), obtaining

(18) ⟨It's a heap⟩ is true or false;

and we can apply (15) to (17), obtaining

(19) ⟨It's a heap⟩ is not determinately true and not determinately false.

Thus we are able to accommodate the phenomenon of vagueness without questioning the law of excluded middle, the principle of bivalence, or the minimalist conception of truth.

Any decent account of vagueness must have something to say about the notorious *sorites* paradox:

(Sor) 0 grains cannot make a heap.
If n grains cannot make a heap, then n + 1 grains cannot make a heap.
∴ For any n, n grains cannot make a heap,

which seems to show, on the basis of incontrovertable premises and impeccable reasoning, that there are no heaps. In so far as we want to give up neither classical logic nor the view that some things are heaps and others are not, then the only remaining option – which I think we can happily embrace – is to deny the second premise. That is, we must allow that there is some unknown (indeed unknowable) number, h, such that h grains cannot make a heap but h + 1 grains can. Thus we are allowing that the predicate 'is a heap' has an extension – albeit an indeterminate one. True, we could not, even in principle, discover the extension. In particular, we could never know the fact of the matter as to whether our little pile is a heap. Such knowledge is precluded by the very meaning of the word – by its being vague. But why should this be thought odd or implausible? It is surely only the lingering seductiveness of verificationism – an inclination to hold that the existence of a fact requires the conceivability of knowing it – that gives rise to discomfort with this situation.[6]

I should stress that the above treatment of vagueness and of

6 Frank Jackson has suggested another possible source of discomfort. He thinks it would be a violation of our sense of symmetry (i.e. the principle of sufficient reason) to suppose that one of the pair of propositions, 'It is a heap' and 'It is not a heap' is a fact and the other isn't, when what we have is clearly a borderline case. However, although I don't doubt that symmetry is appealing, it seems to me that we would rather accept that the world is disappointingly asymmetrical, than abandon classical logic.

the *sorites* paradox has substantial merits and should not be viewed merely as a necessary but rather unwelcome outgrowth of minimalism. In the first place it is not the case that minimalism *dictates* our solution. The situation, rather, is that the deflationary perspective primes us to expect – what could well be recognized independently – that the problems of vagueness are simply not addressed by an account of truth. Once this is appreciated, we can see that the real choice is between the abandonment of classical logic and the abandonment of verificationism. My sentiments in favour of the latter option are independent of minimalism. That response succeeds in preserving the simple and well-entrenched principles of excluded middle and bivalence, offers a positive analysis of vagueness, proposes a way out of the paradox, and gives an explanation of why that way out might have seemed so counter-intuitive. Thus our approach to indeterminacy is not just a biproduct of minimalism, and has a great deal of plausibility in its own right.

Moreover, the rejection of minimalism would be of no help whatsoever in dealing with these matters. For, as we have seen, the only genuine alternative to what is proposed here involves the rejection of classical logic – which is a move not made any less difficult by the adoption of a non-minimalist theory of truth.[7] Moreover, the semantic principle,

7 It is far from clear what the new logic would be. Putnam (1983) suggests intuitionistic logic. However, a 'vagueness logic', in so far as it is motivated by the idea that 'indeterminate truth' is impossible, would need to renounce the inference from the conditional,

k is F $\rightarrow$ k is determinately F,

to its contrapositive,

k is not determinately F $\rightarrow$ k is not F.

Otherwise, in a case where k is evidently a borderline case: i.e.

k is not determinately F and not determinately not-F,

it could be inferred that

k is not F and k is not not-F,

(*continued*)

(E) ⟨p⟩ is true *iff* p,

which binds our logic and metalogic, and which prevents us (on pain of contradiction) from combining classical logic with the thesis that neither ⟨A⟩ nor ⟨−A⟩ is true, is by no means peculiar to minimalism. Just about all accounts of truth subscribe to it. So it certainly cannot be suggested that by adopting minimalism we are depriving ourselves of an easy solution to the problems of indeterminacy.

Finally, it is perhaps worth noting how certain superficially different approaches to vagueness might be partially accommodated to the present point of view. Consider, for instance, an idea of Kit Fine's (1975), endorsed by Dummett (1978), that a sentence containing vague expressions is absolutely TRUE just in case it is true relative to any admissable way of making the vague terms precise. If we take 'TRUE' to mean 'determinately true' then this idea becomes a perfectly consistent and illuminating elaboration of the minimalist view sketched above. But if it is assumed that nothing can be true unless TRUE, as Fine and Dummett are inclined to say, then the result is disaster. For we can infer that neither ⟨A⟩ nor ⟨−A⟩ is true, which implies a contradiction. So the former interpretation is clearly preferable. Another strategy for dealing with vagueness has been to invoke infinitely many TRUTH VALUES: all the real numbers from 0 to 1. The idea is that when a vague predicate, 'F', is applied to a borderline case, n, the resulting TRUTH VALUE is somewhere in the middle between 0 and 1; that the conditional, 'F(n) → F(n + 1)', has a TRUTH VALUE just less than 1; and that the TRUTH VALUE of the conjunction of many such propositions gradually decreases as the number of

– a contradiction. Thus 'vagueness logic' must renounce *contraposition* – a principle which is perfectly acceptable from the intuitionistic point of view. Moreover, there is no reason for a 'vagueness logic' to quarrel with the principle of double negation elimination:

k is not not-F → k is F,

which is intuitionistically *un*acceptable. Thus intuitionism is not the logic of vagueness.

conjuncts increases – reaching 0 when we get to '(n) [(F(n) → F(n + 1)]'. As before, these ideas can be reconciled with the minimalist viewpoint. It suffices to identify 'TRUTH VALUE = 1' with 'determinate truth', 'TRUTH VALUE = 0' with 'determinate falsity', and (perhaps) 'TRUTH VALUE (⟨p⟩) = x' with something like 'proportion x of the linguistic community would judge, in light of full knowledge of underlying conditions, that p'. So far so good. Difficulties arise only if the new TRUTH VALUES, 1 and 0, are identified with truth and falsity. But this step can and should be resisted. In order to eliminate the paradoxes of vagueness it suffices to appreciate, first, that a notion of *determinacy* should be invoked to articulate the nature of vagueness; and, secondly, that this will make it unnecessary to tamper with any of the entrenched laws of logic and semantics, and will enable us to accept with equinamity the falsity of the *sorites*' main premise.

29 There is a substantive issue in meta-ethics as to whether evaluative utterances purport to assert truths or whether they are merely expressions of feeling; but this question would be trivialized by minimalism.

There has indeed been a tendency for ethical emotivists (also known as 'non-cognitivists'), to want to use the notion of truth-value to distinguish 'genuine descriptions' from syntactically similar sentences whose linguistic role is arguably non-descriptive. And this practice certainly is at odds with a minimalist perspective, from which ethical propositions are perfectly good and useful instances of the equivalence schema. But the moral here is not that minimalism and emotivism are incompatible, but that emotivism should be re-formulated. For a minimalist could quite easily accept the correctness and philosophical importance of the emotivists' central insights: namely, that the function and assertibility conditions of certain ethical claims are fundamentally different from those of empirical, explanatory descriptions, and that an appreciation of the difference will help to resolve philosophical problems surrounding the notion of an ethical fact. My point is that this position need not, and should not, be formulated in such a way as to preclude the minimalist conception of truth. More specifically, the emotivist might attempt to characterize the unusual nature of certain ethical propositions by supposing, very roughly speaking, that the meaning of 'X is good' is sometimes given by the rule that a person is in a position to assert it when he is aware that he values X (which is *not* to say that 'X is good' means 'I value X'). This sort of account has some claim to being able to dissolve some of the epistemological problems of ethics and explain why certain ethical beliefs have motivational force. Thus the essential character of emotivism might be captured without having to question the existence of ethical propositions, beliefs, assertions, etc., and without having to deny that they satisfy the usual logical and metalogical principles.

6

Propositions and Utterances

30 Propositions are highly dubious entities. It is unclear what they are supposed to be, and their very *existence* is controversial. Would it not be better, therefore, to develop a theory of truth that does not presuppose them – by assuming, for example, that *utterances* are the primary bearers of truth?

According to the advocate of propositions, whenever anyone has a belief, a desire, a hope, or any of the so-called propositional attitudes then his state of mind consists in there being some relation between him and a special kind of entity: namely, the *thing* that is believed, desired to be the case, hoped for, etc. Thus if Oscar believes that dogs bite, this is alleged to be so in virtue of the obtaining of a relation, *believing*, between Oscar and a certain proposition: namely, *that dogs bite*.

The considerable merit of this theory is that it appears to provide an adequate account of the logical properties of belief attributions and the like. We are inclined to infer from

(1) Oscar believes that dogs bite

to

(2) There is something Oscar believes,

and from

(3) Oscar doubts that it will rain

and

(4) Barnaby is saying that it will rain

to

(5) Oscar doubts what Barnaby is saying.

Such inferences may be subsumed under familiar logical rules provided that apparently singular terms such as

(6) what Barnaby is saying

and

(7) that it will rain

are taken at face value to refer to a species of object – to be called 'propositions'.

It might well be countered, however, that such evidence should not be taken as conclusive. After all, syntax is not an infallible guide to semantic structure. Indeed one of the central concerns of this book – whether the truth predicate does or does not stand for some sort of property – derives from this well known fact. And there are many less controversial examples: e.g. 'Jones' sake', 'The average man', 'Smith's appearance'. The last of these examples is particularly close to the issue at hand. There is a relation of *resemblance* between certain things, but this relation is not transitive: it may be that A looks like B and B looks like C, but A does not look like C. Given this failure of transitivity we cannot suppose that there is a realm of entities, *appearances*, such that every object possesses exactly one of them, which it shares with all the objects it resembles; for that supposition would imply transitivity. Thus although we do express resemblance claims by saying that certain things have the same appearance, it turns out on closer scrutiny of the logical properties of such claims that their structure cannot be what would seem most natural given their syntactic form, namely:

(8) (∃x) (x is the appearance of A and x is the appearance of B).

Similarly, it should not be taken for granted that our ordinary talk of 'what Oscar believes' is to be construed at face-value as referring to a special kind of entity.[1]

In order to clarify this issue, let us step back for a moment from the case of propositions and consider more generally why it is that we impute logical form in the way that we do. The logical forms of the sentences in a language are those aspects of their meanings that determine the relations of deductive entailment holding amongst them. Let us imagine a body of sentences characterized by their concern with a certain range of phenomena; and suppose that we have mounted an investigation into the relations of deductive entailment that hold between these sentences. Suppose that the results of our investigation suggest an attribution of logical forms having the implication that some of the sentences will clearly entail the existence of entities of a certain type – call them 'Ks'. Suppose finally that we believe that some of those sentences express truths. Taken together, these considerations would provide a basis for thinking that things of type K exist. But how powerful are these reasons? Under what circumstances, if any, would it be right to resist them – to maintain that despite the aforementioned evidence there are really no such entities as Ks?

Of course, one thing that would justify resistance would be the discovery that our assignment of logical forms is unsatisfactory. Suppose we found another way of doing it which gave a more complete representation of our inferential practice, and which involved no commitment to Ks. In that case our prior ground for believing in them would be completely undermined.

Another possible source of resistance would be the discovery of non-philosophical arguments for the conclusion that Ks don't exist. In calling these arguments 'non-philosophical' I have in

1 Particular grounds for doubt lie in the possibility that *translation* is affiliated with the notion of *resemblance*, (roughly, via the identification of intertranslatability with resemblance in use), and is infected with its intransitivity. If this were so, then we could not suppose there to be a class of entities such that every attitude-expression is associated with exactly one of these entities, sharing it with all the other attitude-expressions with which it is intertranslatable. Thus the existence of propositions is put in question. This problem is addressed directly in the answer to question 32.

mind that they would come from *inside* the field to which the statements in question belong. Consider for example arguments within physics that the aether does not exist, or arguments within zoology against the Loch Ness Monster. These are evaluated with respect to the same canons of justification that govern the original body of statements. If they are deemed acceptable then the result is a revision in our scientific beliefs; but no change is called for in the logical forms that we attribute to them.

Finally, the most philosophically interesting case is that in which general philosophical considerations motivate a disinclination to postulate Ks. It might be argued, for example, that only *material* objects exist and Ks would not be material; or that sheer ontological parsimony requires us to do without Ks if at all possible; or that, given the nature of Ks, knowledge about them could not be squared with otherwise attractive epistemological theories; or that we would be unable to answer basic questions, such as 'What are Ks?', 'When is K1 the same as K2?', 'Where are Ks?', to which we would have every right to expect answers if Ks really existed.

There are three types of response to any such argument: (a) we may regard it as fallacious, and proceed to explain how this is so; (b) we may find it persuasive, accept that Ks don't exist, and conclude that a certain body of what we used to believe is mistaken; and (c) in order to preserve our earlier scientific beliefs and still be able to accept the conclusion that Ks don't exist, we might abandon the account of logical forms that involves commitment to Ks and replace it with one that doesn't.

Of these alternatives it seems clear that option (a) is always best; for the arguments that it asks us to reject are extremely weak in the first place. Often they involve barefaced overgeneralization of the following sort. First, physical objects are taken to be paradigm examples of what exists; secondly, certain prominent properties of such objects are identified; thirdly, it is inferred that only entities with these properties could exist; fourthly, it is noticed that Ks would not have them; and finally, the conclusion is drawn that Ks cannot exist. Evidently no great conceptual strain is involved in rejecting such arguments, which beg the whole question in their first premise. So option (a) is quite acceptable. The other alternatives, however, exhibit some highly undesirable features. Option (b) implies that we must start denying things that we presently regard as certainly true. Option (c) involves the idea that the correct logical forms are not those that provide a perfectly adequate account of inferential practice. We are to reject a certain way of formulating our beliefs solely because it has features that are irrationally regarded as unwelcome, and even though it accords precisely with our entrenched criteria for being a good formulation.

It is easy to see how these general conclusions will apply to the case of propositions. In the first place we can suppose that an adequate account of the logical forms of belief attribution (and other so-called propositional attitude statements) involves the supposition that 'that p' is a singular term. Thus from 'Oscar believes that dogs bite' we can infer 'Oscar believes something', and this is assimilated to the rule of existential generalization. In the second place, we may assume that some propositional attitude statements are certainly true. For example, it is certainly true that Einstein claimed that matter is a form of energy. Thirdly, we should take these assumptions to entail that there is an entity, *what Einstein claimed*, or in other words, *the proposition that matter is a form of energy*. And fourthly, we should not be troubled by an inability to say *where* this entity is, or *what* it is made of. For such questions are not appropriately asked of things like propositions. Similarly, it should not trouble us that propositions will not enter into causal relations with us, so that our knowing anything about them will violate the 'causal theory of knowledge'. For this theory derives its entire *prima facie* plausibility from the sort of blatantly question-begging overgeneralization mentioned above – in this case, from the unjustified presupposition that everything is known in the same way that physical objects are known.

I conclude that a compelling argument for the existence of propositions may be built on the premise that they participate in an adequate account of the logical forms of belief attributions and similar constructions. Moreover, the required premise appears to be correct. Therefore, despite their peculiarities, we should not balk at propositions and should not object to their use in a theory of truth.

31 The case for propositions assumes the adequacy of a certain logical analysis of belief – one that construes the state of belief as a relation between a person and a kind of entity, the <u>content</u> of the belief. But this assumption is plagued with familiar difficulties and appears to be mistaken.

The main alleged difficulties have to do with a dispute about the nature of propositions – a dispute which goes back to Frege and Russell. Russell (1903) claimed that a proposition consists of the very objects it is about. For example

(9) the proposition *that Hesperus is visible*

would be made up of the object, Hesperus, and the property of *being visible*. If Russell was right then, since 'Hesperus' and 'Phosphorous' have turned out to be two names for the same planet, then

(10) the proposition *that Phosphorous is visible*

is the very same proposition as (9). But how, in that case, do we account for the fact that someone may be aware – as we say, *de dicto* – that Hesperus is visible and not that Phospherous is? In light of this problem Frege (1892) claimed that the proposition expressed by a sentence (what he called a 'thought') is composed of the *senses*, rather than the *referents*, of its constituent words. So (9) and (10) would be different from one another. But if he was right then so called *de re* beliefs become problematic. For surely the discovery about a certain object *that it is Phosphorous* does not consist in a relation between the believer and the tautologous Fregean proposition, ⟨Phosphorous is Phosphorous⟩! The latter belief is trivial whereas the former is not.

One way of dealing with these problems is to acknowledge the existence of *both* Fregean *and* Russellian propositions – the first being the objects of *de dicto* belief, and the second of *de re* belief. The idea is that all propositions have some logical structure (e.g. $\phi(x)$, $\psi(x,y)$, $(x)(\exists y)\,(\phi(x) \rightarrow \psi(x,y))$, etc.), and that each position in such a structure may be filled either by a Fregean sense or by the referent of such a sense. Thus there are pure Fregean, *abstract propositions*, in which a logical structure is filled only with senses; there are pure Russellian, *concrete propositions*, in which a logical structure is filled only with referents; and there are *mixed propositions*, in which some of the locations are occupied by senses and the others by objects. For example, corresponding to the sentence

(11) Hesperus is identical to Phosphorous

there is an abstract proposition which consists of the senses of 'is identical to', 'Hesperus', and 'Phosphorous' embedded, in that order, in the structure '$\psi(x,y)$'; the concrete proposition consisting of the referents of those expressions embedded in that structure, and six different mixed propositions. Therefore,

(12) Raphael believes that Hesperus is Phosphorous

has eight readings[2] – one for each of the propositions to which one might be saying that Raphael is related. Disambiguation is achieved (in English) by use of the qualifier '*of* X' for any of the propositional constituents that are intended to be referents rather than senses. Thus, if one says

(13) Raphael believes *of Hesperus* that it is Phosphorous,

the object of belief is the mixed proposition in which the 'x'-position in '$\psi(x,y)$' is filled by the object, Hesperus, and the other positions are filled with senses. And if one attributes the belief without any such qualification, what is conveyed is a *de dicto* belief – a belief whose object is the purely abstract proposition.

Moreover it seems plausible to suppose that in order to have a *de re* belief *of* something, it is necessary to have in mind a special way of conceiving of the thing – a way that is sufficiently intimate

2 Or perhaps only four readings. Perhaps only the referents of the *singular* terms – in this case, 'Hesperus' and 'Phosphorous' – can be what *de re* beliefs are about.

to constitute 'knowing what the thing is'.[3] Therefore a certain relationship exists between *de dicto* and *de re* belief. In order for someone to believe a proposition that is not entirely abstract (i.e. in order for him to have a *de re* belief), two things are required. First, he must believe some wholly abstract proposition from which the other may be derived by replacing some of the senses with their referents. And, secondly, the believer's conception of these referents must be such as to qualify him as 'knowing what they are'. Admittedly the second condition is vague and context dependent. But this is entirely appropriate, since the set of circumstances in which *de re* belief may properly be attributed is also vague and context dependent.

It seems therefore that *prima facie* difficulties in what would otherwise appear to be the most straightforward construal of belief attributions may be overcome. Beliefs should indeed be analysed as relations between persons and propositions. Thus our practice of belief attribution commits us to the existence of propositions.

32 'The proposition *that p* is true *iff* p' can be thought to capture our conception of truth only if truth is not already presupposed in the very idea of a proposition. But this requirement may well be violated. For a central component of the notion of *proposition* is lodged in the statement of identity conditions for propositions – the conditions for two utterances to express the same proposition. But this is an idea one might plausibly explain in terms of the *inter-translatability* of the utterances, which, in turn, could be construed as their having the same *truth* conditions. And if the concept of truth is needed to say what propositions are, then a theory of truth cannot take propositions for granted.

A complete treatment of this issue would go beyond the scope of this essay. However, I agree that our having the concept of

3 See Hintikka (1962), Kaplan (1969), and Quine (1977) for discussion of this sort of requirement for *de re* belief.

proposition presupposes that we can make sense of claims of the form,

(14) ‘**u** expresses the same proposition as **u***’.

Therefore, it is incumbent on me to say something about the notion of *utterance translation* on which I am relying – at least enough to quell the suspicion of circularity.

The general conception of meaning and translation to which I wish to appeal is the so called ‘use theory’ articulated in various forms by Wittgenstein (1953), Sellars (1954), Quine (1960), Harman (1982, 1987), Peacocke (1986) and many others. Roughly speaking the right translation between the words of two languages is the mapping that ‘best’ preserves overall similarity of usage – where usage is characterized in terms of circumstances of application, contribution to the assertibility conditions and inferential role of containing sentences, etc. Thus it is part of the use of the word ‘red’ in English that it is applied to red things, and that the applicability of ‘coloured’ and ‘not green’ may be inferred from it.[4] What counts as ‘most similar overall’ here is vague and highly context dependent. Therefore Quine’s (1960) thesis of the indeterminacy of translation is sustained. However, this is by no means fatal as far as propositions are concerned. For if there is no determinate fact of the matter as to whether two utterances are inter-translatable, then there is no determinate fact of the matter as to whether they express the same proposition. But as we saw in the answer to question 28, such facts may be indeterminate but none the less exist. Indeterminacy is found throughout our conceptual scheme – whether we are talking about material objects, persons, societies, species, or whatever – and so its presence in the domain of propositions too should be no cause for sceptical concern.

Notice that the ‘languages’ between which utterance translations exist are not languages in the ordinary sense (i.e. English, French,

4 The use theory of meaning bears some resemblance to the ‘conceptual role semantics’ described by Field (1977) and Block (1986). A vital difference, however, is that according to their view the meaning of a word is identified with its *internal mental* role, whereas according to the use theory, as I understand it, the meaning of a word also includes its use in relation to the external world.

etc.). Rather they are versions of such languages, relativized to contexts. Let us call these things 'contextualized languages'. The contextualized language CL(**u**) of a particular English utterance **u** is a version of English in which the word 'I' is a name of the speaker, the word 'here' is the name of a region of space including the speaker, and ambiguous words of English have been given definite senses in accordance with the dispositions of the speaker concerning their use. In order to translate the utterance **u** of CL(**u**) into a sentence **u*** of CL*(**u***) it is necessary to construct a sentence in CL*(**u***) which both has the same logical structure as **u** in CL(**u**) and which has constituents with the same meanings as the corresponding elements of **u**. In other words, each constituent of **u*** must have the same use in CL*(**u***) as the corresponding constituent of **u** has in CL(**u**).

Sometimes it is simply not possible to translate a certain utterance **u** into a given context language CL*. For it might be that no word of CL* has a close enough resemblance in use to the use that some word of **u** has in CL(**u**). This may be the case, for example, if **u** contains the first person pronoun, or the word 'that', or certain other indexicals or demonstratives. However, although we can perhaps find no sentence of CL* that expresses the same *Fregean* proposition as **u**, we might still get the next best thing: namely, a sentence, **u***, of CL* that expresses the same *Russellian* proposition as **u**. In that case we can say that **u*** is a *weak translation* of **u**.

Let me indicate how this general approach deals with some particular cases. If the utterance **u** uses the first person pronoun, then its weak translation, **u***, will contain, in the corresponding position, a name of the speaker of **u**, or else another pronoun (e.g. 'he') that in the context language CL*(**u***) names that individual. Similarly, if the utterance **u** employs the word 'now' then the corresponding element of **u*** will be some expression refering to whatever region of time surrounding **u** was intended by the speaker. This element might also be the word 'now', provided that **u*** occurs at the same time as **u** and that its natural language is English. Otherwise the weak translation of 'now' might be 'maintenant', 'then', 'about 3 p.m.' – it all depends on the contextualized language of **u***. Thus if **u** is an utterance by Pierre at midday on 1 January 1980 of 'J'ai faim' and if CL*(**u***) is a contextualized language involving a different person at a different time speaking English, then **u*** might be 'Pierre was hungry at noon yesterday'.

Considering the matter more systematically, the process of identifying the content of an utterance, **u** – that is, the process of translating **u** into our own current context language – may be broken down into the following stages:

1. Identify the sentence type, S(**u**), and language, L(**u**), with which **u** is uttered.
2. Translate S(**u**) of L(**u**) into a set of alternative sentence types, {S1, S2, . . .}, of the home language, E.
3. Invoke the speaker's intentions to select one – say Sj – of this set of sentence types: what he would have said if he had been speaking language E.
4. For each indexical or demonstrative expression, i, that occurs in Sj, substitute a context-independent term, d, of E (i.e. not indexical and not demonstrative) such that 'i = d' is assertible with certainty in the context of Sj.
5. Utterance of the resulting sentence, Sj*, would be the weak translation in the current contextualized language of the original utterance **u**.

The important point in all this is that the canons of translation are designed to preserve similarity in use, and that use is characterized in terms that do not cite truth. Consequently, propositions are not grasped via the notion of truth; and so we are free to suppose that this notion is entirely captured by the equivalence principle.[5]

33 But the 'use theory' of meaning implies that propositions don't exist. For if *translation* is a matter of resemblance in use, then it is not a transitive relation, and so there can be no such things as 'what inter-translatable utterances have in common'. (Harman, 1973)

Formulated more carefully, this argument against propositions proceeds by comparing the following three principles:

5 For further discussion of this point – specifically the relationship between *understanding a sentence* and *knowing its truth conditions* – see the answer to question 22.

(A) Two utterances express the same propositions just in case they are inter-translatable.

(B) Utterances are inter-translatable just in case they have corresponding constituents with a similar use.

(C) There are words, x, y, and z, such that the use of x resembles the use of y, which resembles the use of z; but the uses of x and z do not resemble one another.

These principles[6] are inconsistent with one another. For the intransitivity of resemblance expressed in (C), combined with the use theory of translation expressed in (B), together entail the intransitivity of translation. But combining this with (A), which says that inter-translatable utterances express the same propositions, we can infer the possibility that u and v express the same propositions, v and w express the same propositions, but u and w do not express the same propositions – which is absurd. Thus, given that relations of resemblance clearly are intransitive, our use theory of meaning entails that the identity conditions for propositions are incoherent, and therefore that propositions don't exist.

My response is to modify premise (B). The use theory of meaning is indeed correct. But the argument shows that premise (B) gives a misleading rendering of it. What we should say instead is that two words are inter-translatable only when they have *the same* use – and not merely *similar* uses. But we must acknowledge that the observable facts of linguistic behaviour, although providing the only possible guide to the existence of this relation of sameness, are not sufficient to establish it objectively. In other words we

6 In formal terms, they are:

A* $(u)(v)(\exists p)(u \text{ express } \langle p\rangle \rightarrow (q)\ ((u \text{ expresses } \langle q\rangle \text{ iff } v \text{ expresses } \langle q\rangle)) \text{ iff } u \text{ trans } v)))$

B* $(u)(v)(u \text{ trans } v \text{ iff } u \text{ has the same structure as } v\ \&\ (n)(x)(y)\{[x \text{ is the } n\text{th constituent of } u\ \&\ y \text{ is the } n\text{th constituent of } v] \rightarrow (\text{use}(x) \text{ in } CL(u)) \text{ resembles } (\text{use}(y) \text{ in } CL\ (v)))$

C* $(\exists x)(\exists y)(\exists z)((\text{use}(x)) \text{ resembles } (\text{use}(y))\ \&\ (\text{use}(y)) \text{ resembles } (\text{use}(z))\ \&\ \text{not } (\text{use}(x)) \text{ resembles } (\text{use}(z)))$

should suppose that although our conception of 'correct translation' is based on our conception of 'two expressions having the same use', none the less it isn't possible to reduce this notion to criteria of resemblance-in-use that may be applied and weighed by every judge in a uniform way. Thus claims of inter-translatability based on similarity of use are not completely determinate. Two people could have equally good grounds for divergent claims and there be no way to settle the matter. So the relation between translation (or 'same use') and observed linguistic behaviour is like the relation between baldness and amount of hair, or between poverty and nett assets. In each case attribution of the former notion can be based only on information about the latter; however there is always a degree of indeterminacy – never an exact rule specifying precisely the conditions in which the former concept applies.[7] None the less, there does exist a fact of the matter. Either two words *are* properly intertranslatable, or they are *not* – even though it may be impossible to say which is so.

I have been trying to rebut an argument designed to show that translation is intransitive – a conclusion that would undermine the existence of propositions. However this rebuttal does not prove that translation *is* transitive. Of course, one way of showing this is to derive it from the existence of propositions. But if one is nervous about propositions precisely on the grounds that translation might be intransitive, then this strategy is no good. An alternative line of thought offering some reassurance goes as follows.

It is implicit in the existence of propositional attitude constructions that a person may adopt a given attitude no matter what the natural language is in which he would express it. We do not regard it as a necessary condition for the truth of

(15) Florence believes that snow is white

that Florence has our language available to her. Moreover we do not suppose that this fact about what Florence believes, if it is a fact, depends on our having characterized it, or on our being able

7 See the answer to question 28 for a discussion of how *indeterminacy* is treated from the minimalist point of view.

to characterize it in the particular way that we did – i.e. in English. One and the same propositional attitude of Florence's may be equally well described in other languages: for example, with

(15-f) Florence croit que la neige est blanche.

But this sort of translatability of propositional attitude attributions implies that translation is transitive. For suppose Florence asserted in a third language some words whose translation into English is

(16) Snow is white,

and suppose that on that basis we English speakers assert (15). If translation were intransitive then there would be no guarantee that

(16-f) La neige est blanche

– which is the translation into French of the translation into English of Florence's words – is the translation into French of Florence's words. So there would be no guarantee that (15-f) manages to characterize the same propositional attitude as (15) does. Thus the assumption that our attributions of propositional attitudes are translatable in the normal way presuppose that translation is transitive.

More formally, suppose **u** and **A** are particular utterances in different languages, and that **A** attributes a certain content to **u** by means of the sentence 'v'. Utterance **A** says in effect that 'v' expresses in the language CL(**A**), what **u** expresses in CL(**u**). Or in other words:

(I) **A** is true *iff* the translation of **u** into CL(**A**) is 'v'.

Suppose, moreover, that *we* would translate the sentence 'v' – as it is used within CL(**A**) – as the sentence 'p'. Then, from our point of view, **A** expresses the statement

(B) **u** expresses the statement that p.

Therefore, **A** is true *iff* **u** expresses the statement that p. In other words,

(II) **A** is true *iff* our translation of **u** is the same as our translation of 'v' from CL(**A**).

Combining (I) and (II) – the two statements of **A**'s truth conditions – we can infer that **u** and 'v'-in-CL(**A**)) are inter-translatable just in case their translations into our language are the same. Therefore, translation is transitive. It can indeed define the equivalence classes with which propositions may be correlated.

34 Many philosophers would agree that if propositions exist then *propositional* truth would be covered by something like the equivalence schema. But they might still maintain that the truth of an *utterance* consists in its 'correspondence with reality', or some other substantive thing. Thus, it is for *utterances* that the deflationary account is controversial, and this position has received no elaboration or defence. (Field, 1988)

Fair enough. So let me now indicate how minimalism deals with the truth of utterances. The initial deflationary impulse is to say that

(D?) Any declarative utterance of the sentence-type 'p', is true if and only if p.

But the trouble with this idea is that different utterances of the same type (e.g. 'I am hungry', 'Banks have money', 'Mary's book is on that table') have different truth values depending on the circumstances in which they are produced and on what is meant by them. Consequently, it is simply false that

(16) *All* utterances of 'I am hungry now' are true *iff I* am hungry *now*,

and similarly for the other examples.

To avoid this difficulty we need a restricted form of the disquotational principle – one in which the way that 'p' is construed when it is *mentioned* on the left-hand side is the same as the way it is construed when it is *used* on the right hand side. In other words, we can endorse instances of the schema

(D′) **u** ∈ ‘p’ → (**u** is true ↔ p),

provided that they – specifically the right-hand sides of the biconditionals – are construed with respect to the same pertinent contextual variables as **u** itself. In other words, an instance of the disquotational schema holds if it is asserted in a context that is not relevantly different from the context of the utterance whose truth is in question.

Implicitly attempting to ensure that this condition is satisfied, Quine (1970) suggests that we restrict instantiation of the disquotational schema to so-called *eternal sentences* – sentences whose tokens exhibit no context sensitivity because they don't contain elements like indexicals, demonstratives and ambiguous words. As for utterances that *are* context-sensitive, Quine proposes to derive each of their truth values from the truth values of ‘equivalent’ eternal sentences. For example, a particular instance of

(17) I am hungry

may be true because of its ‘equivalence’ to the eternal sentence,

(18) Albert Einstein is hungry at noon on 1 January 1947.

However, there are a couple of difficulties with this strategy. In the first place, the problem of context sensitivity is not really solved because the same string of words can appear in several languages and for that reason have different truth values on different occasions. Thus, strictly speaking, there are no eternal sentences. Moreover, as soon as one tries to patch things up by inserting reference to a *language* in the disquotation schema, i.e.

(D+) ‘p’ is true in L *iff* p

then the theory is undermined. For unless something is said about what it is for an utterance to be 'in language L', the schema will becomes a definition of *that* notion rather than a definition of truth. But if we do fill out the modified schema with an account of what it is for an utterance to be 'in language L', then, in effect, the theory will be explaining the truth of utterances in terms of the truth of the propositions they express, and so its distinctively disquotational character will be lost.[8] In the second place, even if we allow Quine's language-relative notion of 'eternal sentence' it is unclear that there would exist enough of them to provide a sufficient basis for the truth-values of all instances of non-eternal sentences. Context sensitivity is by no means restricted to indexicals and demonstratives. Most names, predicates and quantifiers can also be construed in various alternative ways. So much so that it is not easy to find English sentences whose instances must all have the same truth value.[9]

For these reasons I do not follow Quine's approach, but adopt an alternative way of making sure that instances of the disquotation schema are construed in the same way as the utterances whose truth conditions they specify. My strategy is to construct cases of the disquotation schema in which the utterance under discussion is *the very one* that is used to articulate that utterance's truth condition. For example:

(19) The immediately following instance of 'snow is white' is true *iff* snow is white.
(20) I am hungry *iff* the immediately preceeding utterance of 'I am hungry' is true.

Thus the correct form of the disquotational schema is:

(D) This ('p') is true iff p,

where 'This ('p')' refers to the instance of 'p' that occurs on the other side of the biconditional.

For every declarative utterance, **u**, there is a *possible* instance

8 See Putnam (1988) for a forceful presentation of this point.

9 This point was impressed on me by Dan Sperber, Pierre Jacob and François Recanati. See Searle (1979), and Barwise and Perry (1983).

of this schema. That is to say there is a possible utterance consisting of **u** followed by some words (in the language of **u**) that mean '. . . iff **u** is true'. The minimal theory of truth for utterances consists of what is expressed by all such possible utterances. As in the case of propositions, this theory can be specified but defies explicit formulation. Suppose we try to formulate the axioms of the theory in our language. We can begin by instantiating the disquotation schema with utterances of our language. But for utterances in other languages, the relevant disquotation instances will themselves be couched in those other languages; so in order to formulate the axioms concerning those utterances, we have to translate those disquotation instances into our language. For example, suppose a French speaker, Pierre, says

(21) J'ai faim

at noon on 1 January 1980. Then the theory of truth contains the following axiom: whatever would be expressed by a possible utterance consisting of the one that was actually made followed by some words in French meaning '. . . *iff* that utterance of "J'ai faim" is true'. *Our* formulation of this axiom is the weak translation, into our language, of this hypothetical claim, namely:

(22) That utterance of 'J'ai faim' is true *iff* Pierre was hungry on 1 January 1980.

Generalizing this result in an obvious way we can give an alternative characterization of the minimal theory of truth for utterances: namely, as every instantiation of the schema

(D-tr) **u** is true iff p,

where '**u**' is replaced by a singular term refering to an utterance and 'p' is replaced by a sentence of our language that, in our context, would be the strong or weak translation of that utterance. As we saw in our discussion of the minimal theory of propositional truth, legitimate instantiation cannot be restricted to sentences in our *current* language; for then the theory would not cover utterances that are not yet translatable. We must be allowed to instantiate an unspecifiable, unlimited number of future sentences of our language. And, as before, this is part of the reason why the theory cannot be fully formulated.

The minimal theory of truth for utterances is equivalent – *modulo* two further principles – to the minimal theory for propositions. The auxiliary assumptions needed to derive either theory from the other are, first, a minimalist specification of the conditions for an arbitrary utterance, **u**, to *express* a given proposition:

(23) **u** expresses the proposition *that p* ↔ trans(**u**)ϵ 'p';

and, second, a specification of the relationship between truth for propositions and truth for utterances:

(24) **u** expresses the proposition *that p* → (**u** is true ↔ the proposition *that p* is true).

These two schematic assumptions entail:

(25) trans(**u**)ϵ 'p' → (**u** is true ↔ the proposition *that p* is true).

And if we are also given that the translation of **u** is 'p' we can infer

(26) **u** is true ↔ the proposition *that p* is true,

which allows us to derive the equivalence schema for propositions,

(E) The proposition *that p* is true ↔ p,

from the translated disquotation schema, (D-tr), for utterances, and also to derive (D-tr) from the equivalence schema. Thus, the accounts of truth for propositions and for utterances are unified and equally deflationary.

Notice moreover that a slight modification of the preceeding argument allows us to derive a minimal theory of truth for beliefs, claims, insinuations, etc. Instead of the preceeding auxiliary principles governing the relationship between utterances and propositions, we invoke analogous principles relating utterances and propositional attitudes, namely:

(24*) **u** expresses the statement *that p* $\leftrightarrow$ trans(**u**) ϵ 'p'

and

(25*) **u** expresses the statement *that p* $\rightarrow$ (the belief (claim, suggestion, . . .) *that p* is true $\leftrightarrow$ **u** is true).

These principles imply

(26*) Trans(**u**) ϵ 'p' $\rightarrow$ (**u** is true $\leftrightarrow$ the belief (etc.) *that p* is true).

And, as before, given the translation of **u** we can now go easily either from the translated disquotation principle to

(EB) The belief (etc) *that p* is true $\leftrightarrow$ p,

or the other way round.

Ordinary language suggests that truth is a property of propositions, and that utterances, beliefs, assertions, etc., inherit their truth-like character from their relationship to propositions. However, the above derivations show that this way of seeing things has no particular great merit. The truth-like conception for each type of entity is equally minimalistic. And by assuming any one of them we can easily derive the others.

In so far as our aim is merely to understand *our* conception of truth, and not to promote some allegedly better one, then I think we have no choice but to acknowledge that truth is primarily attributed to what we believe, question, suppose, etc. That is to say, truth is applied to the objects of our so-called propositional attitudes. However there are a couple of influential sources of scepticism about this article of common sense – an article wholly embraced by minimalism – and it has been my purpose in this chapter to respond to them. First, many philosophers feel a certain queasiness about recognizing that propositions exist. Therefore I sketched the case in favour of them (based on the logical form of belief attributions) and tried to undermine the usual counter-arguments (which derive from their supposed weirdness and the alleged intransitivity of translation). In the second place, there is a tendency to think that our conception of 'proposition' *presupposes* the notion of truth, so that the minimalist order of explanation would seem to be the wrong way round. And to this I replied that we might employ an account of meaning (hence 'proposition') in terms of *use* – in particular, *assertibility* – which would not require a prior grasp of truth. This idea was already mentioned in the answer to question 22. Finally, for those who are not convinced by these arguments, I showed that minimalist theories of 'truth' for utterances and belief-states can be given without making a commitment to propositions.

7

The 'Correspondence' Intuition

35 Clearly truth is some sort of correspondence with reality; and this is left out of the minimalist account.

It can indeed seem patently obvious that the truth or falsity of a statement is something that grows out of its relations to external aspects of reality. And this sentiment is what lies behind so-called 'correspondence theories of truth'. According to one such theory (Wittgenstein, 1922) the alleged correspondence is between representations and *facts*: the truth of a sentence or proposition is said to derive from the existence of whatever fact it '*depicts*'. Alternatively, there are accounts (e.g. Tarski, 1958; Davidson, 1969) in which the ontological category of *fact* is eschewed, and the truth of a whole is built directly out of the relations of reference and satisfaction between its parts and various external objects. Here, the truth of a thing is engendered by the objects to which its constituents correspond.

Admittedly minimalism does not *explain what truth is* in any such way. But it does not deny that truths *do* correspond – in *some* sense – to the facts. And it does not dispute the existence of relationships between truth, reference and predicate-satisfaction. Thus we might hope to accommodate much of what the correspondence theorist wishes to say without retreating an inch from our deflationary position. Let us see how this can indeed be done.

The line of thought leading to the correspondence theory begins with the innocuous idea that whenever a sentence or proposition is true, it is true *because* something in the world is a certain way

– something typically external to the sentence or proposition. For example

(1) 'Snow is white' is true *because* snow is white.

That is to say

(2) 'Snow is white' 's being true *is explained by* snow's being white.

In other words

(3) The fact that 'snow is white' is true *is explained by* the fact that snow is white.

That is

(4) 'Snow is white' *is made true by* the fact that snow is white.

These observations are perfectly consistent with minimalism. In mapping out the relations of explanatory dependence between phenomena we naturally and properly grant ultimate explanatory priority to such things as basic laws and the initial conditions of the universe. From these facts we deduce, and thereby explain, why, for example

(5) Snow is white.

And only then, given the minimal theory, do we deduce, and thereby explain, why

(6) 'Snow is white' is true.

Therefore, from the minimalistic point of view, (1) is fine. And the other statements are nothing but trivial reformulations of it.[1] Thus we can be perfectly comfortable with the idea that each truth is made true by the existence of a corresponding fact.

36 If truth is constituted from a single correspondence relation to the world, then we should be able to obtain a theory of truth which improves on the undesirable list-like character of the minimal theory.

The correspondence approach becomes distinctive and controversial only at the point that there is an attempt to extrapolate from the list of claims like (4) a general theory of truth: for example, something along the lines of:

(CT) x is made true by y *iff* (y is a fact & x corresponds to y)

x is true *iff* (∃y)(x is made true by y),

where the relation of correspondence holds between, on the one hand, 'snow is white' (and the proposition, ⟨snow is white⟩) and, on the other hand, *the fact that snow is white* – and similarly for other true sentences. However, it is essential to having an *attractive* correspondence theory that there be something more to the relation of *correspondence* than is conveyed by the minimalistic schema

(Cor) (x ∊ 'p' or x = ⟨p⟩) → (x corresponds to y *iff* y = the fact *that p*),

1 In order to get (4) from (1) we must (and, from a minimalist perspective, *can*) assume all instances of

(a) (∃x)(x = the fact that p) *iff* p,

(b) (There is such a thing as the fact that p *because* there is such a thing as the fact that q) *iff* (the fact that p *is explained by* the fact that q),

(c) (The fact that b is F *is explained by* the fact that c is G) *iff* (b *is made* F *by* the fact that c is G).

and something more to *being a fact* than is given by

(F) y = ⟨p⟩ → (y is a fact *iff* p).

For otherwise we would not have improved on the minimal theory. The new theory would be just as 'list-like' and would be best seen as an *extension* of the minimal theory into new domains, rather than as an *alternative* to it. Thus any correspondence theory worthy of the name – any version of the theory that could be presented as an alternative to minimalism – would have to provide non-schematic and unified theories of *correspondence* and *fact*.

Let us consider the prospects for such a theory, bearing in mind some of the different kinds of thing to which truth may be applied – namely, sentence-tokens (arrangements of linguistic expressions), Fregean propositions (arrangements of the *senses* of linguistic expressions), and Russellian propositions (arrangements of the *referents* of linguistic expressions, given their senses).[2]

As an account of truth for Russellian propositions the correspondence approach seems wholly inappropriate. For it is clear that such propositions, when true, would be *identical* to facts, and not in any sense merely 'similar' to them. In other words, for Russellian propositions,

(7) ⟨p⟩ is true

simply means

(7*) ⟨p⟩ is a fact.

Therefore, our problem in this case is to give a *single* theory of *being true* and *being a fact*; and our best bet appears to be the minimalist schema

(E+) ⟨p⟩ is a fact ↔ ⟨p⟩ is true
↔ p.

Turning to Fregean propositions, there are two ways to go. One

2 The two types of proposition were introduced, in the answer to question 31, as the objects of *de dicto* and *de re* belief.

option is to maintain that they also, when true, are identical to facts. This idea may come from the feeling that, for example, the fact that Phosphorous is Hesperus is *not* identical to the fact that Phosphorous is Phosphorous. Thus we might countenance both Fregean and Russellian facts – two types of true proposition. And once again we would be excluding the possibility of a substantive correspondence theory.

Alternatively one might suppose that any Fregean proposition – and a sentence would presumably be treated in the same way – is made true by the existence of the corresponding *Russellian* fact. This, in effect, is Wittgenstein's (1922) 'picture theory'. The rough idea here is that a sentence-token (or a Fregean proposition) consists of elements arranged in a certain logical form, and the fact that this is so *depicts* that there is in reality a Russellian fact consisting of the referents of the elements arranged in the same logical form as in the sentence. The sentence is true if there is such a fact and false if there isn't. Formulated more precisely, the theory would look something like this:

(PT) If S is a sequence of expressions (or senses) and O is a sequence of entities (of the same length as S) then S refers to O iff (n) (the nth member of S refers to the nth member of O).

x corresponds to y iff (\$) (S) ({\$ is a logical form
& S is a sequence of elements
& x exhibits \$
& x involves S} →
(∃O) {O is a sequence of entities
& S refers to O
& y exhibits \$
& y involves O})

y = ⟨p⟩ → (y is a fact iff p).
x is true iff (∃y) (x corresponds to y and y is a fact)

But although these principles are quite plausible and certainly worth noting, they do not make a good alternative to the minimal theory. The single respect in which the minimal theory can seem unattractive is its infinite, list-like character. Sellars (1962) compares it to a telephone directory. And precisely this feature is preserved in the picture theory, since, in effect, a separate axiom is needed for each instance of 'p'. In addition, a theory of reference is required; and as we saw in the answer to question 5 there is reason to think that this too would require infinitely many axioms. And this is not yet to mention the need for theories of what it is for a fact to *exhibit* a logical form, and for a fact to *involve* a certain sequence of entities. Thus if we were to trade minimalism for the picture theory we would sacrifice purity and simplicity for absolutely no benefit. This implies that, although its principles may well be correct, the picture theory of truth should not be thought to qualify as our *basic* theory of truth.

Thus we have failed to find any correspondence account of truth possessing methodological virtues lacked by the minimal theory. No doubt one may formulate interesting, plausible schema that relate the concepts of truth, fact and correspondence. But the conjunction of such schematic principles is best viewed as a legitimate extension of our theory of truth; it does not provide a tempting alternative.

37 Certain cases of representation (e.g. by maps) clearly involve a correspondence – a structural resemblance – to what is represented. So is it not reasonable to expect some such relation in linguistic representation also?

Perhaps so. However, it remains to be shown, for either type of representation, that such structural similarities are in any way *constitutive* of truth. The minimalist view is that they are not.

The difference between a map (or any so-called 'realistic' representation) and a sentence of a natural language is that the interpretation of maps is more 'natural' – or in other words, less 'conventional' – than the interpretation of a sentence. Let me explain what I mean by this. In the case of certain maps, a representation that consists in some set of objects (symbols) standing in some relation to one another is supposed to be interpreted as saying that the referents of those objects stand in that very same relation. For example,

(8) The fact that *point y* is on a straight line between *points x* and *z*

expresses

(9) The fact that *the place represented by y* is on a straight line between *the places represented by x* and *z*.

Thus what is special about 'realistic', 'natural', 'non-conventional' systems of representation is that they have syntactic features (e.g. one thing being on a line between two other things) that refer to *themselves*. In other words, facts (8) and (9) share, not merely logical form, but also a certain pictorial form: namely,

(10) That . . . is on a straight line between . . . and . . .

This suggests that we could construct a theory of truth for pictorial representations that would parallel the theory of truth for sentences, (PT), given above – the only difference being that the variable '$' would range over pictorial forms instead of logical forms. However, although this is indeed possible, the result would be just as cumbersome as (PT) turned out to be, and just as unsatisfactory compared to the minimalist theory. So, even for pictorial representations, the best theory of truth is the minimal theory.

This assumes, of course, that the minimal theory can be applied to pictures; and let me quickly show that this is so. According to minimalism, the axiom of the theory of truth relevant to any particular representation, R, is expressed by a possible instance of the disquotational schema, formulated in the language of R. In order to express this axiom in *our* language we must of course translate it from the language of R. For example, the axiom for

(11) Schnee ist weiss

is initially expressed by the disquotational biconditional

(12) 'Schnee ist weiss' ist zwar *wnn* schnee ist weiss

which, as we would say, expresses the proposition

(13) 'Schnee ist weiss' is true *iff* snow is white.

And similarly, the truth condition of a map,

(M) | A——B———C |

is given by its translation into English:[3] namely,

(14) M is true *iff* B is between A and C.

Thus we are able to articulate the difference and similarity between linguistic and pictorial representation, and show that in neither case is a relation of correspondence, or structural similarity, involved in an account of its truth.

38 The minimal theory fails to show how the truth of a sentence depends on the referential properties of its parts.

Another substantial account of truth that is sometimes regarded as an elaboration of the 'correspondence theory', is the Tarski-inspired compositional approach.[4] Tarski's account resembles the picture theory in that the truth of a sentence is explained in terms of the semantic properties of its constituents. But it differs from the picture theory in not explicitly referring to facts or to logical structures. It is ontologically simpler, but formulationally more complex than the picture theory. This is because instead of

3 Of course the 'map language' is not rich enough to contain a disquotational axiom for M (or for anything else). Nevertheless we can imagine an enrichment that would permit such a representation and we can say what its English translation would be.

4 It is unclear that Tarski himself would endorse this construal of his work. Davidson (1969), however, has argued that it should be seen as vindicating the correspondence intuition. Note also that Tarski's (1958) own initial theory of truth was not given for languages containing names, and does not reduce truth to reference but solely to predicate-satisfaction. Nevertheless, the following points apply to it.

quantifying over logical forms in a single principle it involves a series of separate clauses for alternative logical forms. Thus, roughly speaking and simplifying enormously, we get:

(TT) u is true-in-L *iff*

(1) u has form '$\phi(x)$' and $(\exists x)$ (Predicate(u) is true-in-L of x & Subject(u) refers-in-L to x)
or (2) u has the form 'p&q' and each conjunct of u is true
or (3) u has the form '$-p$' and what is negated in u is not true
or (4) u has the form . . .

which can ultimately be turned into an explicit definition of truth.

Tarski himself was content to show that for certain simple languages, L, he could define a predicate, 'true-in-L', the extension of which would be the truths of L. But someone (e.g. Davidson, 1969) might hope to go further and arrive at a general theory of truth by, first, showing, even for complex, natural language such as English, that 'true-in-L' could be defined in terms of 'refers-in-L' and 'satisfies-in-L'; and second, defining plain 'truth' for an utterance, u, as the existence of an utterance, v, of the home language, E, such that *v is the translation into E of u* and *v is true-in-E*.

However, there are two basic objections to any such approach. In the first place, as Davidson himself concedes, the Tarskian strategy applies only to those sentences whose logical forms may be represented in first order logic. Or, in other words, it applies only to those sentences whose truth values are determined by the truth values of atomic sentences. But there is no reason to assume that every conceivable truth has such a structure. Consider, for example, counterfactual conditionals, probability claims, laws of nature, and modal assertions of various kinds. All of these constructions resist formalization in the language of predicate logic, and so it would appear that Tarski's theory does not cover them.

In the second place, as we saw in the answer to question 5, such a theory of truth will be adequate only if it is supplemented with theories of reference and satisfaction; and these require either substitutional quantification, or an unformulatable collection of axioms. So no simplification is achieved by reducing truth to reference and satisfaction. On the contrary, the extreme conceptual purity and simplicity of minimalism is thrown away for nothing. The correspondence approach promised to rectify a certain perceived defect of minimalism: namely its infinite, list-like character – its failure to say what all truths have in common. But it turns out that some of the terms to which truth is to be reduced are similarly intractable; and so the initial promise of correspondence is not fulfilled.

In rejecting the idea that the correspondence theory describes the basic nature of truth, we are denying that truth, reference and satisfaction are constitutively interdependent on one another. But we are certainly not trying to suggest that the semantic principles relating those matters are incorrect. We are supposing, rather, that such principles should not be treated as explanatorily basic, but should each be explained in terms of simple, separate minimal theories of truth, reference and satisfaction. And in fact this can be done very easily. For example, it is not a part of our basic theory of truth that we should accept instances of,

(15) 'p and q' is true *iff* 'p' is true and 'q' is true.

However, this is trivially deducible from

(i) 'p and q' is true *iff* p and q,
(ii) 'p' is true *iff* p,

and

(iii) 'q' is true *iff* q.

Similarly, we do not define truth in terms of reference and satisfaction using such principles as

(T/R) 'Fa' is true *iff* (∃x) ('a' refers to x & 'F' is satisfied by x).

However this schema is easily explained. For we have

(S′) (x)(x satisfies 'F' *iff* Fx)

and

(R′) (x)('a' refers to x *iff* a = x).

Therefore the right-hand side of (T/R) is equivalent to

(16) Fa,

which, given the disquotational principle, is equivalent to the left-hand side of (T/R),

(17) 'Fa' is true.

Thus the minimal theory does not preclude the possibility of showing how the truth-value of a sentence is related to the referential properties of its parts.

The best theory of truth will be the smallest, simplest collection of statements that, in conjunction with theories of other matters such as reference, will enable us to derive everything we believe about truth. This desideratum points us towards minimalism and away from theories, such as Tarski's, which are unnecessarily complex, explanatorily misguided, and foster the misleading impression that truth, reference and satisfaction are inextricably intertwined with one another.

39 The great virtue of defining truth in terms of reference is that the account may be supplemented with a naturalistic (causal) theory of the reference relation to yield, in the end, a naturalistic and scientifically respectable theory of truth. (Field, 1972; Devitt, 1984).

The usual line on singular reference goes roughly as follows. Once upon a time we believed the description theory of Frege (1892) and Russell (1905). It was held that every time a name is used it is intended to be synonymous with some definite description.

Thus 'Socrates' may, in some idiolect, mean 'the teacher of Plato'. This idea was refined by Wittgenstein (1953) and Searle (1958) who argued that a name, though perhaps not synonymous with any particular definite description, is none the less associated with a certain cluster of definite descriptions which jointly determine what it stands for. But, so the story goes, this whole picture of reference has been decisively refuted by Kripke (1972). Suppose, to give one of his examples, an obscure mathematician, Schmidt, was really the person who discovered the incompleteness of arithmetic, although Gödel has been unfairly given the credit. In that case, even if someone's only belief expressed by means of the name 'Gödel' were that Gödel discovered the incompleteness of arithmetic, we would none the less say that his uses of the name do not refer to Schmidt, but to Gödel. Kripke used such counter-examples to the description theory in order to motivate an alternative 'causal' picture of the reference relation. The idea here is that there is a certain type of causal chain connecting the uses of a name and the thing it stands for. What remains, according to this line of thought, is to formulate a definite theory of reference that would manage to capture this causal picture – but unfortunately no-one has been able to do it yet.

From the minimalist perspective this failure comes as no surprise. For truth and reference are so intimately related that the rationale for a minimal account of truth will equally well motivate a minimal account of reference. Reference, on this view, is not a complex relation; a naturalistic or conceptual reduction is not needed and should not be expected.

Notice, moreover, that Kripke's own model contains nothing to preclude some role for *representation* in the fixing of a name's referent; and the introduction of names by means of initial modes of presentation (demonstrative or descriptive) is not given a non-semantic analysis. His central claim is merely that there need be no reference-fixing characterization in the minds of users of the name. For as use of the name spreads 'causally' through a linguistic community, the initial modes of presentation might well be lost. But this is merely an instance of a quite general point about meaning, applying to all words, and not just to names. The point is that the meaning of an expression is not intrinsic to the minds of individual language users but resides in the practices of the linguistic community as a whole and is properly attributed to an individual on the basis of his interactive relations with the community (see Burge, 1979). Thus what is 'causal' in Kripke's theory has nothing specifically to do with names, and the term 'causal theory of names' is quite misleading in connection with his discussion. One shouldn't think that he gives even so much as a *crude* version of a causal theory of reference.

Such a conception becomes even less plausible when it is combined, as it often is, with the thesis that names have no meaning (i.e. no Fregean sense) and that their only possible contribution to the propositions they help to express is their referent. As we saw in the answer to question 31 this position makes it impossible to give a satisfactory account of *de dicto* propositional attitudes (which at least the description theory was able to do). Moreover it appears to be the product of an over-reaction to Kripke's arguments. Granted they show that names do not have the same meanings as definite descriptions; but this provides no reason to conclude that names have no meanings at all. We might suppose, rather, that they are *primitive* expressions. And there would be no mystery about this. After all, most predicates are primitive; so why shouldn't names be as well?

As in the case of singular terms the search for a causal theory of predicate satisfaction (for example, by Stampe, 1977; Dretske, 1981; and Fodor, 1987) is conducted as if it were perfectly obvious that there is such a thing and all that remains is to work out the details. But this obviousness, this sense that from a naturalistic, scientifically respectable viewpoint such an account *must* be right, has its origin in the same linguistic illusion that motivates substantive theories of truth. Therefore the continual failure of its advocates to produce an adequate theory is only to be expected.[5]

Paralleling our approach to truth, minimalist accounts of satisfaction and reference would begin with a story about the *function* of those notions. Roughly and briefly, one might suppose that just as truth helps us to talk about propositions that are

5 See T. Blackburn (1988) for a discussion of the failed attempts. As he says, 'it is remarkable that the "new approach" is still so much discussed and cited, when so little has been done to redeem those enthusiastically penned promisory notes which marked its inception'.

wholly unarticulated, so satisfaction and reference help us to talk about propositions of which certain *parts* – those corresponding, respectively, to predicates and singular terms – are unarticulated. Just as truth performs its function by providing a sentence of *our* contextualized language,

(18) 'X' is true,

which is equivalent to the utterance

(19) 'X',

which might be in *any* language, so satisfaction and reference do their jobs because

(20) satisfies 'F'

and

(21) the referent of 'D'

provide *home language* equivalents of any predicate, 'F', or singular term, 'D', whatever their language, and whether or not their translations are available. Moreover, just as truth is a convenient alternative to substitutional quantification into sentence positions, so satisfaction and reference enable us to do without substitutional quantification into predicate and singular term positions. Thus instead of

(22) $\{\phi\}$ (x) (ϕx v-ϕx)

one can say

(22*) Given any predicate and any object, either the object satisfies the predicate or it doesn't,

and instead of

(23) $\{\exists d\}$ (Raphael's belief contains $\langle d \rangle$ and d = the moon)

one can say

(23*) The referent of a constituent of Raphael's thought is the moon,

or

(23**) Raphael is thinking about the moon.

Having characterized the 'non-descriptive' roles of 'satisfies' and 'refers', the second stage of a minimalist account of satisfaction and reference is to specify the theories that would suffice for the performance of these functions. Paralleling the theory of truth, these would be, respectively, every proposition of the form

(S) $(x)(x \text{ satisfies } \langle F \rangle \leftrightarrow Fx)$,

and every proposition of the form

(R) $(x)(\langle d \rangle \text{ refers to } x \leftrightarrow d = x)$.

Given such an explanation of the behaviour and purpose of our notions of reference and satisfaction it would be a very surprising coincidence if there were unified conceptual or naturalistic reductions of these phenomena.[6]

The correspondence conception of truth involves two claims: (a) that truths correspond to reality; and (b) that such correspondence is what truth essentially is. And the minimalist response, urged in this chapter, is to concede the first of these theses but to deny the second. The rationale for this response is that the minimalistic equivalence axioms can easily be supplemented with plausible characterizations of *correspondence* and *fact* to show that, indeed, any true proposition or sentence is made true by some fact. However, we have also seen that there are no advantages – and substantial disadvantages – in supposing that this entire

6 Arguments for the basic character of the minimal theories of reference and satisfaction may be constructed in parallel to the arguments, given in the answer to question 14, for the basic character of the minimal theory of truth.

construction constitutes the basic theory of truth. One merely imaginary benefit is that a correspondence account, by reducing truth to reference and reference to causation, would leave us with a finite, naturalistic model – and thereby make the concept of truth scientifically respectable. I argued, however, that *reference*, *satisfaction*, *correspondence* and *fact* are just as non-naturalistic, and in need of infinite, deflationary theories, as truth is. Moreover, such theories are *already* perfectly legitimate from a scientific point of view, without any additional naturalistic reduction. Therefore the extra notions employed in the correspondence theory do not earn their keep, and merely introduce unnecessary complexity. Ordinary canons of explanatory priority dictate that the trivial equivalence principles be taken as fundamental, and that further characteristics of truth, including its correspondence properties, be accounted for on the basis of that theory.

Conclusion

Although the minimalist point of view has been subjected to many objections, we have seen that it is by no means incapable of dealing with them. Indeed from this trial it emerges even stronger than before. For we now have a clear formulation of the doctrine, a coherent set of replies to a very broad range of criticisms, a picture of the alternative accounts and what is wrong with them, and a sense of the theory's significant philosophical implications.

Let me end by summarizing the line of thought that has been pursued here. We began with just about the only uncontroversial fact to be found in this domain: namely, that the proposition *that snow is white* is true *iff* snow is white, the proposition *that tachyons exist* is true *iff* tachyons exist, and so on. We then posed, and attempted to answer, two questions about this general fact. First, what precisely is it? Can we provide a clear and logically respectable characterization of it – one which does not rely on improper locutions, like 'and so on'? Secondly, is there any further, deeper, non-trivial theory of truth – some account going beneath or beyond instances of the equivalence schema? With respect to the descriptive question I argued that a theory containing all the equivalence principles cannot be formulated – unless notions are employed that themselves require unformulatable theories. This is because there are too many axioms, and also because some of them concern propositions that we cannot yet express. On the question of whether any further theory of truth remains to be found my answer was a categorical no. Hence the name 'minimalism'. The justification for this answer fell into a couple of parts. I argued, in the first place, that all uses of the truth predicate are explained by the hypothesis that its entire *raison d'être* is to help us say things about unarticulated propositions, and in particular to express generalizations about them. It transpired in the course of the book that our apparently deep uses of truth in logic, semantics, and the philosophy of science are simply displays of this role. Secondly, I showed that the performance of this function requires nothing more or less than the truth of the equivalence axioms. Thus minimalism perfectly explains all the pertinent facts; and that is its justification. As for the philosophical import of minimalism, this should no longer be in doubt. We have seen that many controversies – regarding, for example, scientific realism, meaning, vagueness, normative emotivism, and the foundations of logic – are standardly assumed to interact essentially with the nature of truth. To the extent that the notion of truth is clarified and its *independence* of these problems established, they can be certain to receive clearer formulation and be more amenable to resolution.

Bibliography

Austin, J. L. (1950) 'Truth', *Proceedings of the Aristotelian Society*. Supplementary vol. 24, 111–128.

Ayer, A. J. (1935) 'The Criterion of Truth', *Analysis*, 3.

—— (1936) *Language, Truth and Logic*, London, Gollanz.

—— (1963) 'Truth', *The Concept of a Person and Other Essays*, London, Macmillan.

Baldwin, T. (1989) 'Can There Be a Substantive Theory of Truth?', *Récherche sur la philosophie et le language*, 10, Grenoble, Université des Sciences Sociales de Grenoble.

Barwise, J. and Perry, J. (1983) *Situations and Attitudes*, Cambridge, Mass., MIT Press.

Black, M. (1948) 'The Semantic Definition of Truth', *Analysis*, 8.

Blackburn, T. (1988) 'The Elusiveness of Reference', *Midwest Studies in Philosophy*, 12, ed. P. French, T. Uehling and H. Wettstein, Minneapolis, University of Minnesota Press.

Blanshard, B. (1939) *The Nature of Thought*, vol. 2, London, Allen and Unwin.

Block, N. (1986) 'Advertisement for a Semantics for Psychology', *Midwest Studies in Philosophy*, 10, ed. P. French, T. Uehling and H. Wettstein, Minneapolis, University of Minnesota Press.

Bradley, F. H. (1914) *Essays on Truth and Reality*, Oxford, Clarendon Press.

Brandom, R. (1984) 'Reference Explained Away', *Journal of Philosophy*, 81, 469–92.

—— (1988) 'Pragmatism, Phenomenalism and Truth Talk', *Midwest Studies in Philosophy*, 12, ed. P. French, T. Uehling and H. Wettstein, Minneapolis, University of Minnesota Press.

Burge, T. (1979) 'Individualism and the Mental', *Midwest Studies in Philosophy*, 4, ed. P. French, T. Uehling and H. Wettstein, Minneapolis, University of Minnesota Press.

Cartwright, R. (1987) 'A Neglected Theory of Truth', *Philosophical Essays*, Cambridge, Mass., MIT Press.

Cohen, J. (1950) 'Mr Strawson's Analysis of Truth', *Analysis*, 10, 136–44.

Davidson, D. (1967) 'Truth and Meaning', *Synthese*, 17.

—— (1969) 'True to the Facts', *Journal of Philosophy*, 66.

—— (1984) *Truth and Interpretation*, Clarendon Press, Oxford.

Devitt, M. (1984) *Realism and Truth*, Princeton, Princeton University Press.

Devitt, M. and Sterelny, K. (1989) *Language and Reality*, MIT Press.

Dewey, J. (1916) *Essays in Experimental Logic*, Chicago, Henry Holt & Co.

—— (1938) *Logic: The Theory of Inquiry*, New York.

Dretske, F. I. (1981) *Knowledge and the Flow of Information*, Cambridge, Mass., MIT Press.

Duhem, P. (1954) *The Aim and Structure of Physical Theory*, Princeton, Princeton University Press. (First published in 1906).

Dummett, M. (1959) 'Truth', *Proceedings of the Aristotelian Society*, n.s. 59; reprinted in *Truth and Other Enigmas*.

—— (1975) 'What is a Theory of Meaning? Part I', in *Mind and Language*, ed. S. Guttenplan, Oxford, Clarendon Press.

—— (1976) 'What is a Theory of Meaning? Part II', in *Truth and Meaning: Essays in Semantics*, ed. G. Evans and J. McDowell, Oxford, Clarendon Press.

—— (1977) *Elements of Intuitionism*, Oxford, Clarendon Press.

—— (1978) *Truth and Other Enigmas*, Oxford, Clarendon Press.

Ezorsky, G. (1963) 'Truth in Context', *Journal of Philosophy*, 60.

Field, H. (1972) 'Tarski's Theory of Truth', *Journal of Philosophy*, 69, 347–75.

—— (1977) 'Logic, Meaning and Conceptual Role', *Journal of Philosophy*, 74, 379–409.

—— (1986) 'The Deflationary Conception of Truth', *Fact, Science and Morality*, ed. G. MacDonald and C. Wright, Oxford, Blackwell.

Fine, A. (1984) 'The Natural Ontological Attitude', *Scientific Realism*, ed. J. Leplin, Berkeley, University of California Press.

Fine, K. (1975) 'Vagueness, Truth and Logic', *Synthese*, 30.

—— (1987) *Psychosemantics*, Cambridge, Mass., MIT Press.

Forbes, G. (1986) 'Truth, Correspondence and Redundancy', *Fact, Science and Morality*, ed. G. MacDonald and C. Wright, Oxford, Blackwell.

Fraassen, B. van (1980) *The Scientific Image*, Oxford, Clarendon Press.

Frege, G. (1891) 'On Function and Concept', in *Translations from the Philosophical Writings of G. Frege*, by M. Black and P. Geach, London and New York, 1960.

—— (1892) 'On Sense and Reference', in *Translations from the Philosophical Writings of G. Frege*, by M. Black and P. Geach, London and New York, 1960.

—— (1918) 'The Thought', trans. A. Quinton and M. Quinton, *Mind*, 65 (1956).

Friedman, M. (1979) 'Truth and Confirmation', *Journal of Philosophy*, 76, 361–82.

Grover, D. Camp, J. and Belnap, N. (1975) 'A Prosentential Theory of Truth', *Philosophical Studies*, 27.

Gupta, A. (1982) 'Truth and Paradox', *Journal of Philosophical Logic*, 11, 1–60. Reprinted in *Recent Essays on Truth and the Liar Paradox*, ed. R. L. Martin, Oxford, Clarendon Press (1984).

Harman, G. (1973) *Thought*, Princeton, Princeton University Press.

—— (1974) 'Meaning and Semantics', in *Semantics and Philosophy*, ed. M. K. Munitz and P. Unger, New York, New York University Press.

—— (1982) 'Conceptual Role Semantics', *Notre Dame Journal of Formal Logic*, 23, 242–56.

—— (1987) '(Nonsolipsistic) Conceptual Role Semantics', in *New Directions in Semantics*, ed. E. LePore, London, Academic Press.

Hempel, C. (1935) 'On the Logical Positivist's Theory of Truth', *Analysis*, 2(4), 49–59.

Hintikka, J. (1962) *Knowledge and Belief*, Ithaca, Cornell University Press.

Horwich, P. G. (1982a) 'Three Forms of Realism', *Synthese*, 51.

—— (1982b) *Probability and Evidence*, Cambridge, Cambridge University Press.

—— (1991) 'On the Nature and Norms of Theoretical Commitment', *Philosophy of Science*, 58.

Inwagen, P. van (1988) 'On Always Being Wrong', *Midwest Studies in Philosophy*, 12, ed. P. French, T. Uehling, and H. Wettstein, Minneapolis, University of Minnesota Press.

James, W. (1909) *The Meaning of Truth*, New York, Longmans Green.

Kaplan, D. (1969) 'Quantifying In', *Words and Objections*, ed. D. Davidson and J. Hintikka, Dordrecht, Reidel.

Kripke, S. (1972) 'Naming and Necessity', *Semantics of Natural Language*, ed. D. Davidson and G. Harman, Dordrecht, Reidel.

—— (1975) 'Outline of a Theory of Truth', *Journal of Philosophy*, 72.

Kuhn, T. S. (1962) *The Structure of Scientific Revolutions*, Chicago, University of Chicago Press.

Leeds, S. (1978) 'Theories of Reference and Truth', *Erkenntnis*, 13.

Loar, B. (1987) 'Truth Beyond All Verification', *Michael Dummett*, ed. B. Taylor, Nijhoff, Dordrecht.

Moore, G. E. (1899) 'The Nature of Judgment', *Mind*, n.s. 8.

—— (1910/11) Lectures, in *Some Main Problems of Philosophy*, London, Allen and Unwin Ltd., 1953.

Papineau, D. (1987) *Reality and Representation*, Oxford, Blackwell.

—— (1991) 'The Problem of Representation', in *Explanation*, ed. D. Knowles, Cambridge, Cambridge University Press.

Peacocke, C. (1986) *Thoughts*, Oxford, Blackwell.

Peirce, C. S. (1932/3) *Collected Papers*, vols 2–4, Cambridge, Mass., Harvard University Press.

Popper, K. (1962) *Conjectures and Refutations*, New York, Basic Books.

Putnam, H. (1978) *Meaning and the Moral Sciences*, London, Routledge and Kegan Paul.

—— (1981) *Reason, Truth and History*, Cambridge, Cambridge University Press.

—— (1983) 'Vagueness and Alternative Logic', *Philosophical Papers, Vol. III: Realism and Reason*, Cambridge, Cambridge University Press.

—— (1988) *Representation and Reality*, Cambridge, Mass., MIT Press.

Quine, W. V. (1953) *From a Logical Point of View*, Cambridge, Mass., Harvard University Press.

—— (1960) *Word and Object*, Cambridge, Mass., MIT Press.

—— (1970) *Philosophy of Logic*, Englewood Cliffs, Prentice-Hall.

—— (1977) 'Intensions Revisited', *Midwest Studies in Philosophy*, 2.

Ramsey, F. (1927) 'Facts and Propositions', *Proceedings of the Aristotelian Society*, Arist. Supplementary vol. 7.

Rorty, R. (1982) *Consequences of Pragmatism*, Minnesota, Minnesota University Press.

Russell, B. (1903) *The Principles of Mathematics*, New York, Norton.

—— (1904) 'Meinong's Theory of Complexes and Assumptions', *Mind*, n.s., 13. Reprinted in D. Lackey (ed.), *Essays in Analysis*, New York, Braziller (1973).

—— (1905) 'On Denoting', *Mind*, n.s. 14.

Searle, J. R. (1958) 'Proper Names', *Mind*, 63, 266, 166–73.

—— (1979) 'Literal Meaning', *Expression and Meaning*, Cambridge, Cambridge University Press.

Sellars, W. (1954) 'Some Reflections on Language Games', *Philosophy of Science*, 21, 204–28.

—— (1962) 'Truth and "Correspondence" ', *Journal of Philosophy*, 59.

Soames, S. (1984) 'What is a Theory of Truth', *Journal of Philosophy*, 81.

Stampe, D. W. (1977) 'Toward a Causal Theory of Linguistic Representation', *Midwest Studies*, vol. 2.

Strawson, P. (1950) 'Truth', *Proceedings of the Aristotelian Society*, Supplementary vol. 24.

—— (1964) 'A Problem About Truth – A Reply to Warnock', in *Truth*, ed. G. Pitcher, Englewood Cliffs, N.J., Prentice-Hall.

Tarski, A. (1943/44) 'The Semantic Conception of Truth', *Philosophy and Phenomenological Research*, IV, pp. 341–75; reprinted in *Readings in Philosophical Analysis*, ed. H. Feigl and W. Sellars, New York, 1949.

—— (1958) 'The Concept of Truth in Formalized Languages',

Logic, Semantics, Metamathematics: Papers from 1923 to 1938, Oxford, Oxford University Press, 152–278.

Thomson, J. F. (1948) 'A Note On Truth', *Analysis*, 8, 67–72.

Warnock, G. (1964) 'A Problem about Truth', *Truth*, ed. G. Pitcher, Englewood Cliffs, N.J., Prentice-Hall.

Williams, M. J. (1986) 'Do We (Epistemologists) Need A Theory of Truth?', *Philosophical Topics*, 14.

Wittgenstein, L. (1922) *Tractatus Logico-Philosophicus*, London, Routledge and Kegan Paul.

—— (1953) *Philosophical Investigations*, Oxford, Oxford University Press.

Wright, C. (1987) 'Further Reflections on the *Sorites* Paradox', *Philosophical Topics*, 15(1), 227–90.

—— (1988) 'Realism, Anti-realism, Irrealism, Quasi-realism', *Midwest Studies in Philosophy*, 12, ed. P. French, T. Uehling and H. Wettstein, Minneapolis, University of Minnesota Press.

Ziff, P. (1962) *Semantic Analysis*, Ithaca, Cornell University Press.

Index